Instructor's Manual

Instructor's Manual
to Accompany

THE
LITTLE, BROWN
HANDBOOK

SECOND EDITION

Prepared By

Robert A. Schwegler
UNIVERSITY OF RHODE ISLAND

Jane E. Aaron

Little, Brown and Company
BOSTON   TORONTO

ISBN 0-316-28978-7

9 8 7 6 5 4 3 2

ALP

Published simultaneously in Canada
by Little, Brown & Company (Canada) Limited

Printed in the United States of America

The authors would like to thank Ann Marie Rapuano, Robert Soderlund, Karen Murphy, Mary Harrington, and Lisa Soderlund for permission to quote from their papers and Times-Mirror Cable Television for permission to quote from its flyer.

Preface

Whatever use you plan to make of The Little, Brown Handbook and whether you are a new teacher or an experienced one, you should find this Instructor's Manual a useful guide to the Handbook and a source of activities and ideas for teaching composition. Chapter 1 of the Instructor's Manual discusses ways to organize a composition course and suggests how the Handbook might be used with different course designs or with other texts such as a rhetoric, a reader, or The Little, Brown Workbook. In addition, the chapter shows how the Handbook's sentence-combining activities can be used to enrich a course. Chapter 2 is a detailed guide to the text that explains the rationale behind each of its chapters and indicates ways they can be adapted to student needs. The chapter also suggests activities and assignments to supplement the exercises in the text. Chapter 3 shows how the Handbook can be an aid in evaluating student papers. Chapter 4 provides a selective, annotated bibliography of resources for teaching composition, covering each of the major topics dealt with in the Handbook and other related subjects such as sentence combining, testing and evaluation, and setting up a writing lab. Following Chapter 4 are the answers to the exercises in The Little, Brown Handbook.

We would like to thank Barbara Carson, University of Georgia, for the answers to exercises that were retained from the first edition and Sue Warne for her aid and guidance in preparing this manual.

CONTENTS

Chapter 1 <u>The Little, Brown Handbook in the Composition Course</u>   1
Organizing the Composition Course   2
Using the <u>Handbook</u> with Other Texts   6
Sentence Combining with <u>The Little, Brown Handbook</u>   9
Tutoring with <u>The Little, Brown Handbook</u>   11

Chapter 2 <u>A Guide to The Little, Brown Handbook: Activities and Assignments</u>   13
The Arrangement of the Handbook   13
Part I   The Whole Paper and Paragraphs   14
Part II   Grammatical Sentences   27
Part III   Clear Sentences   36
Part IV   Effective Sentences   43
Part V   Punctuation   47
Part VI   Mechanics   49
Part VII   Effective Words   49
Part VIII   Special Writing Assignments   52
Appendixes and Glossaries   54

Chapter 3 <u>Evaluating Student Essays</u>   57
Three Approaches to Commenting on Papers   57
Making Sure Students Understand Your Comments   62
Focused, Positive Commentary   64
Evaluating Essays for a Grade   68
Evaluating for Revision   80
Peer Grading and Conferences   81

Chapter 4 <u>Teaching Composition: A Selective Bibliography</u>   85
General Works   87
The Whole Paper and Paragraphs   90
Sentences   98
Words, Punctuation, and Mechanics   101
Special Writing Assignments   102
Evaluation/Peer Grading   104
Sentence Combining   106
Setting Up a Writing Lab   107

ANSWERS TO THE EXERCISES   109

Part I THE WHOLE PAPER AND PARAGRAPHS   111
Chapter 1   Developing an Essay   111
Chapter 2   Writing and Revising the Essay   119
Chapter 3   Composing Good Paragraphs   121
Chapter 4   Convincing a Reader   128

Part II GRAMMATICAL SENTENCES   134
Chapter 5   Understanding Sentence Grammar   134
Chapter 6   Case of Nouns and Pronouns   145
Chapter 7   Verb Forms, Tense, Mood, and Voice   146
Chapter 8   Agreement   149
Chapter 9   Adjectives and Adverbs   151

Part III CLEAR SENTENCES   155
Chapter 10   Sentence Fragments   155
Chapter 11   Comma Splices and Run-on Sentences   157
Chapter 12   Pronoun Reference   160
Chapter 13   Shifts   161
Chapter 14   Misplaced and Dangling Modifiers   164
Chapter 15   Mixed and Incomplete Sentences   166

Part IV EFFECTIVE SENTENCES   168
Chapter 16   Using Coordination and Subordination   168
Chapter 17   Using Parallelism   172
Chapter 18   Emphasizing Main Ideas   174
Chapter 19   Achieving Variety   177

Part V PUNCTUATION   180
Chapter 20   End Punctuation   180
Chapter 21   The Comma   181
Chapter 22   The Semicolon   187
Chapter 23   The Apostrophe   191
Chapter 24   Quotation Marks   194
Chapter 25   Other Punctuation Marks   196

Part VI MECHANICS   199
Chapter 26   Capitals   199
Chapter 27   Italics   199
Chapter 28   Abbreviations   200
Chapter 29   Numbers   201
Chapter 30   Word Division   202

Part VII EFFECTIVE WORDS   203
Chapter 31   Controlling Diction   203
Chapter 32   Using the Dictionary   209
Chapter 33   Improving Your Vocabulary   209
Chapter 34   Spelling   211

Part VIII SPECIAL WRITING ASSIGNMENTS   213
Chapter 35   Writing a Research Paper   213

CHAPTER 1

THE LITTLE, BROWN HANDBOOK IN THE COMPOSITION COURSE

The Little, Brown Handbook can be a valuable resource
for composition teaching, partly because of its flexibility.
There are almost as many different ways to organize a composition course as there are skills involved in successful
writing. Writing is a complex act, drawing together many
skills including the ability to produce acceptable sentences
and paragraphs, the ability to discover and organize ideas,
and the ability to reach a compromise between the aims of
personal expression and the needs of an audience. No wonder,
then, that when the time comes to organize a course, a
composition instructor faces a host of questions: Should self
expression or critical thinking be the goal of the course?
Should it emphasize the forms of expression and thought, the
mental operations that help produce good writing, or the
richness of content that makes an essay worth reading? What
units should the course contain and which should come first?
Just as there is no single right answer to these and the
many other questions an instructor faces, so there is no
perfect way to organize a composition course. Writing and
the teaching of writing are simply too complex and contain
too much overlap to allow for simple answers. Most instructors, for example, recognize the need to help students become
proficient in the mental operations we call the "writing
process"; yet, instructors also know that knowledge of the
possible forms for expression--the features of the finished
product--is itself an important component of the writing
process. And while it is true that a successful essay begins
with good sentences and paragraphs, the sentences and paragraphs are likely to be good only if the writer understands
where the essay as a whole is going.

1

The <u>Handbook</u> in Composition Courses

ORGANIZING THE COMPOSITION COURSE

Organizing a composition course means choosing to
emphasize those aspects of writing that the instructor (or
the department) considers most important and that meet students' needs. At the same time, it means figuring out a way
to include in the course the other aspects of successful
writing. In recent years, composition teaching has followed
three general patterns for organizing a course: emphasis on
patterns of expression and thought, emphasis on the writing
process, and emphasis on content and ideas. Each approach
can be successful if it meets the needs of a particular group
of students and if the instructor pays some attention to all
aspects of composing, not merely those emphasized by the
course design. And each approach can easily accommodate <u>The
Little, Brown Handbook</u>.

Emphasis on Patterns of Expression and Thought

Many instructors believe that a composition course ought
to give students a chance to understand and practice basic
patterns of expression and thought. Courses may vary widely,
however, in the patterns they emphasize: rhetorical and
logical patterns (classification, comparison-contrast, deduc-
tion), essay structures (thesis and support, general to specific), patterns of paragraph development, and sentence patterns. Such courses have in common two assumptions about the
way students learn to write: first, that by understanding and
mastering the elements of a finished essay, students will be
able to improve their writing; and, second, that patterns of
expression can act as patterns of thought in that they help a
writer to understand, shape, and communicate experience.
The first assumption predominates in what might be
called <u>skills courses</u>, often designed to serve developmental
students or students who have difficulty writing whole
essays. Skills courses focus on developing sentence and
paragraph skills, moving to the whole essay only after students have mastered different kinds of paragraphs. Instructors who choose this approach generally argue that the basic
sentence pattern of subject + assertion and the standard
paragraph pattern of subject + assertion + support are simply
smaller versions of the thesis + support pattern of whole
essays and the assertion + support pattern of thought characteristic of much expository writing, particularly in academic settings. Thus, skills courses not only try to break
the task of academic writing into manageable units, they also
help introduce patterns of thought essential to success in
college courses.

2

In organizing a skills course, you might begin with a unit on sentence structure, drawing on Chapters 5 to 9 of the <u>Handbook</u> ("Grammatical Sentences"), and you might stress an understanding of phrases, clauses, basic sentence types, and verb forms and tense. Along with this, or beginning later in the semester if appropriate, you might require paragraph-length writing and make use of the extensive discussion in Chapter 3 ("Composing Good Paragraphs"). Paragraph-length writing can continue throughout the semester accompanied by work in Chapters 10 to 15 ("Clear Sentences") and 16 to 19 ("Effective Sentences"). Starting with paragraphs as early as possible can give students a sense of accomplishment and a chance to put into practice what they are learning in the sentence units. Chapters on punctuation, mechanics, diction, and usage can be assigned whenever they meet the needs of the class or of individual students.

While an effective skills course can focus on sentence, paragraph, and essay patterns, it also needs to pay attention to the writing process and to audience (Chapters 1, 2, and 4 in the <u>Handbook</u>). Students who have trouble mastering the basic forms of expression are also likely to underestimate the importance of prewriting and revision and to have difficulty shaping their writing to the needs of an audience. These matters need to be covered and reinforced throughout the course, perhaps through assignments that require prewriting and revision and also create realistic audiences and situations for students to address in their writing.

The other assumption behind the emphasis on patterns of expression and thought—that patterns of expression can also be ways of viewing experience—leads to what might be called rhetorically oriented courses. Instructors who teach this sort of course sometimes focus primarily on surveying basic essay types (narration, description, exposition, and argument) or patterns of development (classification, analysis, comparison-contrast). Yet they may also view the patterns of development as patterns of thought as well as expression, and they may introduce the patterns as a means of probing subjects and developing and organizing essays. Regardless of their approach, these instructors share the belief that students who have understood the patterns and practiced them in their writing will be able to make use of them in a variety of writing tasks. Most of these instructors would also agree that each pattern of development directs attention to a different aspect of a subject. In this way, the patterns can be seen as shaping the way we think about a subject and as affecting the attitudes of a reader.

If you wish to give your course a rhetorical orientation, you may want to begin with Chapters 1 to 4 of the <u>Handbook</u> ("The Whole Paper and Paragraphs") as a way of showing students how to develop, write, and revise an essay and to adapt it to an audience. Later in the course, you may want to return to this material to remind students of the importance of the stages of the writing process, particularly prewriting and revision. You can also point out that Chapters 1 and 3 treat the rhetorical patterns as answers to questions about aspects of a topic as well as ways to organize and develop essays and paragraphs. The main portion of the course might consist of a review of essay types or patterns of essay and paragraph development (Chapters 1 to 3) with assignments that give students a chance to use the forms. The chapters on coordination and subordination, parallelism, sentence emphasis, and variety (Chapters 16 to 19, "Effective Sentences") can be introduced later in the course to add variety and style to the students' writing. The chapters on common sentence errors, punctuation, mechanics, diction, and usage can be assigned according to the needs of individuals or of the class and may also be used for reference. The course might culminate in a research paper (Chapter 35) or with memos and essay questions (Chapter 36).

Rhetorically oriented courses often rely on a reader or rhetoric to provide examples of essay types and patterns of development. The danger in a rhetorically oriented course is that students will come to regard the various forms as ends in themselves and ignore the role they play in viewing experience and in shaping communication to an audience or situation. For this reason, many instructors emphasize the process of exploring subjects and revising the plan for an essay throughout the course, and they try to create specific audiences and situations for students to address in their writing.

Emphasis on the Writing Process

Many instructors believe that a composition course should emphasize the process of writing rather than the forms writing can take. This approach assumes that by helping our students respond to writing situations with a full awareness of the importance of each element in the writing process—prewriting, writing, and revising—and by giving them a chance to adapt the process to demands of different kinds of writing, we enable them to respond to future writing tasks in an effective way. A <u>process oriented</u> course does not ignore the forms of expression but presents them instead as strategies best learned in the context of a particular writing task. It also assumes that matters of grammar, punctuation, and mechanics are learned most readily when they are necessary for effective communication in an essay.

In organizing a course that emphasizes the writing process, you might begin by having students look over the discussion of the process in the <u>Handbook</u> (Chapters 1 and 2, "Developing an Essay," "Writing and Revising the Essay"). You will, of course, have to make a brief review of the writing process a part of each assignment, both to remind students of the importance of each of the elements of composing and to show how the kinds of planning and revising a writer must do will vary slightly depending on the subject, the aim of the writing task, and the audience for the essay. You may wish to start the course with personal writing because it turns attention inward and often makes students aware of how their minds operate as they write. When you move to more public kinds of writing, however, Chapter 4 ("Convincing a Reader") will help alert students to the need to take their readers into account as they shape what they have to say and decide how to say it.

The assignments in a process-oriented course should stress the importance of prewriting and revision in all writing tasks. They also should suggest writing strategies students can use to deal with a subject and meet the needs of a reader. If the assigned essay requires particular attention to paragraphing—a persuasive paper, for example—then the assignment or the class work that accompanies it might require students to look at Chapter 3 ("Composing Good Paragraphs"). Chapters 16 to 19 ("Effective Sentences") will also help introduce students to useful strategies, and Chapters 35 ("Writing a Research Paper") and 36 ("Practical Writing") can be good resources when students are asked to write academic papers or memos directed at a business or professional audience. Coverage of matters of grammar, punctuation, diction, and usage will depend on the needs of the class and of individual students.

Since many problems in student writing can be traced to a lack of effective prewriting or revision, a composition course that emphasizes process can have a significant impact on student writing. But students need to be aware of the strategies that make for good writing, too: strategies in word choice, sentence structure, paragraph development, and essay organization. Therefore, a course that emphasizes the writing process needs to introduce students to stylistic options and to their usefulness in communicating the writer's purpose to an audience.

Emphasis on Content and Ideas

Courses that emphasize ideas and essay content—often called <u>thematic courses</u>—generally rest on the beliefs that

the best kind of writing grows out of a strong need to communicate and that students are most likely to have a desire
to communicate when they are exposed to significant ideas and
issues. The ideas and issues around which such a course is
built may be personal—family life, education, or social
relationships—or they may be matters of public policy—the
environment, pornography, or the American legal system. The
sources for the course content may be a reader, a lecture
series, films, or the students' own research and experiences.
Whatever the particular design of such courses, it is the
course content and not the writing process or the forms of
writing that receives the primary focus. This does not mean
that instructors who teach such courses place little value on
writing. Instead, they generally consider a piece of writing
important for what it has to say, and they view the forms of
writing and the writing process as important only to the
extent that they enable the writer to communicate ideas and
feelings clearly and effectively.

If you choose to emphasize essay content in your composition course, you may wish to begin by introducing students to the writing process and the basic forms of the essay
through Chapters 1 to 4, "The Whole Paper and Paragraphs."
These chapters suggest ways students can develop their ideas
and organize them into paragraphs and whole essays. As
students struggle to express their ideas, you may wish to
assign Chapters 31 to 34 ("Effective Words") to help them
communicate more precisely and Chapters 16 to 19 ("Effective
Sentences") to help them add variety, clarity, and style to
their writing. Chapters on punctuation, mechanics, grammar,
and usage can be assigned to the class or to individual students according to need. If students are required to use
research in their writing, Chapter 35 ("Writing a Research
Paper") will be helpful.

USING THE HANDBOOK WITH OTHER TEXTS

Although The Little, Brown Handbook can be used as the
only text in a course, many instructors also adopt a reader,
a rhetoric, or a workbook like The Little, Brown Workbook.
Each kind of text enables the instructor to give different
emphasis to the course and also provides activities to help
students develop their writing.

With a Reader

Readers are generally of two kinds: rhetorical and
thematic. Rhetorical readers provide selections from pro-

fessional authors and sometimes student writing arranged to illustrate the different aims and patterns of writing. Readers of this type frequently begin with writing patterns that students find most accessible--narration, description, exemplification--and move on to patterns students find more difficult to use--classification, comparison-contrast, inductive and deductive argument. Many readers provide extensive introductions to the rhetorical patterns, discussing their uses in writing and the aspects of a subject they focus on. Thematic readers, in contrast, present groups of writings illustrating and exploring a number of themes, such as the stages of personal growth or family relationships or topics of general interest like the women's movement, capital punishment, or the controversy over pornography. The writings, which may include fiction or poetry as well as essays, usually represent a range of perspectives on the subjects; and they are often accompanied by background information. Some readers are both rhetorical and thematic in organization and coverage and provide two tables of contents, one with a rhetorical arrangement, the other following a thematic plan.

Both types of readers can be used to generate class discussion and topics for student writing. Some readers even provide questions to stimulate discussion and lists of possible paper topics. If the sole purpose of using the reader is to provide subject matter for essays, a thematic reader may be preferable because, as a rule, readers of this type provide several perspectives on a subject and more background information to get class discussion started and give students material to use in their writing.

Rhetorical readers, and some thematic readers too, can be sources of model essays that illustrate, among other things, patterns of development, essay and paragraph strategies, variety in tone, and sentence emphasis and variety. The questions accompanying the essays in most rhetorical readers direct students' attention to the most important features of the models and suggest ways the students can incorporate such features in their own writing.

Instructors who adopt a reader typically make discussion of its essays a major activity of the course, yet they also tend to make significant use of a handbook. If the reader chosen for a course does not provide a rhetorical framework for students' essays or thorough coverage of the writing process, instructors using <u>The Little, Brown Handbook</u> may wish to direct students to the coverage of these matters in Chapters 1, 2, and 4. The <u>Handbook</u> provides explanations and examples of other matters frequently not covered by readers, such as paragraphing (Chapter 3); sentence structure, grammar, and style (Chapters 5 to 19); diction and usage (Chapters 31 to 33, Glossary of Usage); and the research paper

(Chapter 35). In addition, the Handbook can be used as a reference for punctuation and mechanics, an aid in marking student papers, and a guide for revision. Some instructors who use a reader like to devote one period each week to subjects covered in the Handbook; others like to set aside part of each day.

With a Rhetoric

Rhetorics cover many of the same topics as handbooks—prewriting, writing, revision, rhetorical patterns, and paragraphing—but they do so in greater depth, at the same time giving much less coverage to grammar, punctuation, mechanics, and usage. A rhetoric usually embodies a particular perspective toward writing and the teaching of writing. It may provide special coverage of the writing process or emphasize thesis-and-support and other standard essay strategies. It may concentrate on personal writing, on argument, on developing tone and style in writing, or on writing across the curriculum. Since a rhetoric thus helps determine the emphasis within a course, it provides less flexibility for the teacher than the Handbook does, especially if the rhetoric has been chosen by a department rather than by the instructor. Yet a rhetoric can provide more extensive coverage of particular areas than is possible in a handbook.

Since rhetorics provide full coverage in some areas at the expense of others, instructors frequently adopt a handbook as a supplement. Used in this way, The Little, Brown Handbook can provide a treatment of sentence style (Chapters 16 to 19) and the research paper (Chapter 35) for those rhetorics that give only brief attention to these matters. It can also provide discussion and exercises for sentence structure and grammar (Chapters 5 to 15), punctuation and mechanics (Chapters 20 to 30), and diction and usage (Chapters 31 to 33, Glossary of Usage). The discussions of paragraphs, the essay, and the writing process (Chapters 1 to 3) can supplement the material in a rhetoric and provide useful exercises.

When the Handbook is used along with a rhetoric, instructors often assign readings and exercises in it at the same time they assign chapters in the rhetoric, and they devote class time to discussing both texts and reviewing the exercises. They also use the Handbook as a reference for students, as an aid to grading papers, and as a guide for revision.

With the Handbook's Ancillary Publications

When combined with its ancillary publications--The
Little, Brown Workbook and its Instructor's Manual, Diagnostic Tests of Standard Written English to Accompany The
Little, Brown Handbook, and this Instructor's Manual, the
Handbook is the center of an instructional package that will
meet the needs of many classes. The diagnostic tests provide
a way for instructors to determine their students' needs at
the beginning of a course and to design the course accord-
ingly. Because the tests are keyed to the different sections
of the Handbook, instructors can decide what chapters in the
text need the most emphasis. (The tests can also be used to
place students in different courses or levels within an
entire composition program.)

The Workbook is designed to give students more extensive
practice with fundamentals than the Handbook alone can provide. Since each section of the Workbook opens with a brief,
simplified version of the discussion in the Handbook, the
Workbook can be used on its own. Yet because each section
corresponds to the treatment of the same subject in the Handbook, the Workbook can be a source of individual and class
activities to complement the primary text. Answers for exercises in the Handbook and the Workbook are published as separate booklets that instructors can order, free, for their
students.

Chapter 2 of this manual describes many activities for
class discussion, small-group work, and individual preparation, each keyed to a particular section of the Handbook. As
a result, then, the entire handbook package can be the basis
for a composition course designed to meet the needs of a
variety of students.

SENTENCE COMBINING WITH THE LITTLE, BROWN HANDBOOK

During the last decade, extensive research has shown
that having students work with the elements of sentences--
manipulating, combining, and altering--leads not only to a
greater understanding of sentence structure but also to a
greater command of options for expression. Best of all, students who practice sentence combining develop a willingness
to use the structures emphasized in the exercises, and their
writing begins to display the kind of flexible, expressive
syntax characteristic of mature writing.

The Little, Brown Handbook contains several kinds of
sentence-combining exercises. Some ask students to combine
two short (kernel) sentences so that the new sentence displays the grammatical or stylistic feature being emphasized

in a chapter. Others ask students to combine sentences to produce a longer sentence following the pattern illustrated by a model sentence. And still others ask students to combine sentences to form a paragraph.

While the sentence-combining exercises can be assigned at any point in the semester, they are most likely to have a positive effect on students' writing when they are part of an ongoing program of sentence combining. When sentence combining is made a regular part of in-class work or out-of-class work each week for an entire semester, it can have a significant effect on student writing, greater even than an intense two-to-three-week session of sentence combining.

Students can begin a sentence-combining program by working with simple exercises like those in Chapter 5, "Understanding Sentence Grammar." Though some of the exercises in this chapter may seem a bit basic for many classes, the ones dealing with appositives and absolutes will acquaint students with features they have probably used little in past writing. From the basic exercises, students can move on to those that introduce relatively complex sentence strategies, and they can conclude their work with paragraph-length exercises. The list below suggests a sequence for a sentence-combining program and identifies chapters in the <u>Handbook</u> that contain appropriate exercises. If you decide to make sentence combining a substantial part of your composition course, you may want to supplement the exercises in the text by making up your own. This will undoubtedly be necessary if your students discover that they like discussing and comparing the results of the exercises in class and want to spend a good deal of time on the activity. Chapter 2 of this manual contains suggestions for sentence-combining activities, and the bibliography in Chapter 4 contains a number of entries on the subject.

A Sequence for Sentence Combining

Chapter 5 "Understanding Sentence Grammar," Exercises 9, 11, 13, 14, 16, 17, 18, 22

Chapter 6 "Case of Nouns and Pronouns," Exercise 4

Chapter 11, "Comma Splices and Run-on Sentences," Exercise 3

Chapter 14 "Misplaced and Dangling Modifiers," Exercise 6

Chapter 21 "The Comma," Exercises 2, 4, 6

Chapter 22 "The Semicolon," Exercises 2, 4, 6, 8

Chapter 16 "Using Coordination and Subordination," Exercises
1, 3, 4, 7

Chapter 17 "Using Parallelism," Exercise 3

Chapter 18 "Emphasizing Main Ideas," Exercises 2 and 4

Chapter 19 "Achieving Variety," Exercises 1, 2, 3

Chapter 3 "Composing Good Paragraphs," Exercises 3 and 9

Chapter 5 introduces students to basic sentence structures, and Chapters 14 and 21 introduce modifying clauses and
phrases along with their primary focus on grammar and punctuation. Chapters 21 and 22 present strategies of coordination as well as of punctuation, and Chapters 16 and 17 introduce progressively more sophisticated sentence strategies.
In Chapter 18 and 19 students encounter sentence patterns
characteristic of mature writing, and in Chapter 3 they get a
chance to combine all the strategies in paragraphs.

TUTORING WITH <u>THE LITTLE, BROWN HANDBOOK</u>

Writing labs and other tutoring services can make good
use of the <u>Handbook</u> and its entire package. The <u>Handbook</u> can
be used to provide explanations and exercises for students,
of course, but it can perform several other valuable functions. It can help resolve conflicts over points of grammar
and usage by being a primary reference, the final arbiter in
debates. It can be a training manual for new tutors, providing simple and clear explanations of problems they will
encounter every day. And it can be a reference for students
who are working on a paper in the lab without the direct
supervision of a tutor.

The <u>Diagnostic Tests of Standard Written English to
Accompany The Little, Brown Handbook</u> can be used to screen
students as they come to the lab, identifying their writing
problems and helping the tutor choose appropriate instructional materials. The <u>Little, Brown Workbook</u> can provide the
"raw material" of tutoring—sample sentences, exercises, and
brief explanations—to be used in discussion with the student
or for independent work. The <u>Workbook</u> can be particularly
effective for tutoring if students are taking composition
courses that use the <u>Handbook</u>, because the language, rules,
and exercises encountered in tutoring will be consistent with
those encountered in the classroom.

CHAPTER 2

A GUIDE TO THE LITTLE, BROWN HANDBOOK:

ACTIVITIES AND ASSIGNMENTS

The aims of this chapter are simple and limited:
first, to comment on the Handbook's organization, coverage,
special features, and possible uses; second, to suggest
assignments and activities that can be used with each different section of the text; and, third, to mention some ways
the Handbook's ancillaries might be used.

THE ARRANGEMENT OF THE HANDBOOK

The Handbook is organized to enhance its usefulness as
a reference while also making it easy to use as a class text
with varied syllabi. The book begins with an overview of
the whole writing process to emphasize the ultimate goal of
almost any composition course--the finished paper. From
there the focus becomes increasingly sharp: a chapter on
paragraphs, fifteen chapters on sentences, four chapters on
words. The arrangement has a certain logic for class work
but doesn't interfere with finding information quickly. In
addition, it also places all the sentence chapters together.

The final chapters contain a thorough treatment of the
research paper, with some practical kinds of writing (essay
examinations, business letters and memos, job applications),
and with appendixes on topics that don't fit in the main-
stream of the text (plagiarism, manuscript form, study
skills). The book ends with two glossaries (usage and
terms) and, of course, with an index.

A Guide to The Little, Brown Handbook

PART I THE WHOLE PAPER AND PARAGRAPHS

Chapters 1 and 2 "Developing an Essay"; "Writing and
    Revising the Essay"

The first two chapters in the Handbook actually constitute a single unit. Together they trace the entire process of writing an essay, from locating a topic to proofreading the final manuscript. The chapters emphasize
throughout the need for a sense of purpose in composing, the
need to be aware of the possible forms for expression, and
the importance of revision. Chapter 1 deals with essay
development—the steps to take before writing a complete
draft of a paper. These are often called prewriting activities, although many of them involve putting a pen to paper
to record ideas or plans for an essay. Chapter 2 begins
with the writing of the first draft and follows its gradual
revision into a final draft.

We all know, of course, how tangled and varied the
writing process is, and we know that experienced writers
usually do not adhere to the neat sequence of steps presented in composition textbooks, including this one. In
reality, writing is circular rather than linear. Each decision changes at least slightly all previous decisions, and
in the middle of drafting an essay a writer may discover the
need to develop new supporting ideas, to make major changes
in the organization, or to shift the purpose of the essay
and modify the thesis. Student writers, however, are often
unaware of all the stages of successful composing and may
shortchange some and skip others entirely. To many students, for example, revision means little more than proofreading, and their first drafts and final drafts are virtually identical. Moreover, few students come to their college composition courses knowing the value of prewriting—
bringing a topic into clear focus, accumulating details and
ideas to develop that topic, determining the central point
or thesis, focusing on an audience, and organizing material.

Thus, whatever your approach to teaching composition
and whenever in the course you plan to deal with whole
essays and paragraphs, you will probably want to emphasize
the composing process. Chapters 1 and 2 separate and discuss the stages of successful composing so that students can
recognize them and understand their importance. At the same
time, the recurrent discussions of student Linda Balik's
paper, traced from an initial vague idea through a final
draft, reinforce the idea of writing as an integrated process. You may find it useful to involve a class in prewriting, working through at least part of the process in

Chapter 1 to give students a concrete understanding of how an essay evolves. You may also find it worthwhile to review with students the practical suggestions for writing and rewriting in Chapter 2 by following the development of Linda Balik's essay as she balances the importance of following the plan established through prewriting with the need to remain open to fresh ideas that occur during writing. The chapter also shows how Balik develops a critical sense toward her own work, sensing flaws in her plan for the paper, responding to the needs of her potential audience, and making use of her instructor's comments.

Chapter 1 begins by alerting students to the different purposes of writing and to the four basic kinds of essays: narrative, descriptive, argumentative, and expository. For classes using a thematic reader, this discussion, along with those about essay patterns later in the chapter and paragraph patterns in Chapter 3, can provide a sound rhetorical framework. Classes using a rhetorically organized reader will find these materials a valuable supplement. The chapter presents various methods for limiting a subject and generating ideas—filling a page, making a list, asking questions—allowing students to discover the techniques that work best for them. The advice for grouping ideas, arriving at a thesis, and organizing an essay likewise encourages a flexible approach to composing. For those students and instructors who find outlining a valuable tool, the chapter provides an extensive discussion followed by exercises designed to help students achieve unity and coherence in their writing. The treatment of audience and tone helps students understand how the purpose of an essay and its audience affect the choices a writer makes. It can also provide a basis for discussion of model essays drawn from a reader. Finally, the discussion of how to organize an essay introduces basic patterns students can use to bring order to their papers, and these strategies correspond to the basic paragraph patterns discussed in Chapter 3. The essay patterns can also help students understand the organization of model essays.

Linda Balik's essay in Chapter 2 follows the comparison and contrast pattern, which is frequently used in writing assignments. Like most student papers, Balik's early draft requires structural revision as well as changes in phrasing and correction of errors in grammar, usage, punctuation, and spelling. The process by which this early draft is turned into a final version is fully illustrated in the chapter to encourage students to make revision a regular part of their writing. Special features of this chapter are the revision checklist students can use for their own papers and the final draft of Balik's essay with instructor's corrections and

comments. The instructor's corrections of the full essay
(pp. 49–51) use the number-and-letter correction code of the
Handbook, and one paragraph is also marked with marginal
comments and correction symbols (p. 52). To familiarize
students with the use of the Handbook, you can assign Exercise 2 in Chapter 2, which asks them to revise Balik's essay
making use of the instructor's comments. You can also use
some of the strategies suggested in Chapter 3 of this
Instructor's Manual ("Making Sure Students Understand Your
Comments"), or you may ask students to read the introduction
to the Handbook, "Using This Book." The two additional student papers at the end of Chapter 2 of the Handbook are
appropriate for class discussion and criticism, as are the
sample papers in Chapter 3 of the Instructor's Manual. Of
course, you may prefer to reproduce representative papers by
your own students for class discussion and analysis.

Activities and Assignments

   1. Identifying Purpose and Mode. Use paragraphs drawn
from magazine articles, from essays in a reader, or from
student papers as a basis for class discussion of the purposes and modes of writing. You may ask students to compare
the aims of individual paragraphs to the overall purpose of
the essays from which they are taken and to decide what role
the paragraphs play within the essay.

   2. Journals. Ask students to keep a journal for ten
days to two weeks, writing for ten to fifteen minutes a day.
Encourage them to record or remember experiences and feelings or to explore ideas and opinions. To make sure the
journals contain different kinds of writing, ask the students to devote a certain number of entries to specific
tasks such as describing a scene, exploring feelings about a
controversial topic, or creating a character sketch of a
friend. The journal entries can later be developed into
formal essays. Journals can also be used to record responses to essays and literary works or to develop reactions
to newspaper articles and television news programs. When
used in this way, journals can be a preparation for critical, argumentative, or expository essays.

   3. Activities That Suggest Topics and Content for
Papers. (a) Check with your audiovisual center or a film
rental service for short films that deal with values or
controversies. The films or the discussions that follow can
become the basis of student papers. (b) Set up class pre-
sentations or debates on an issue in order to provide infor-

mation and sharpen the focus for papers dealing with the issue or with related topics. (c) Ask students to look at a variety of magazines and to bring in a list of the topics covered in their articles. The topics may in turn suggest topics for student essays. The exercise can be extended by asking students to summarize the contents of one or more of the articles and to indicate how the content might appeal to a particular audience. (d) Ask students to take a notebook with them to some place likely to be filled with activity and vivid sense impressions--a laundromat, the center of the campus, a busy restaurant. They should record their impressions of the scene in the notebook and later turn it into a structured descriptive essay or use the material in some other kind of essay.

4. <u>Places to Find Topics</u>. To help students discover interesting topics, suggest places they can look in their experiences, among their ideas, or in the world around them. For narrative essays, you might suggest that students look at experiences like these:

> sports and contests, camping and fishing trips, accidents and fires, graduations, vivid childhood experiences, embarrassing moments like giving a speech in school, frightening moments like getting lost in a city or a department store, robberies, and public events

For descriptive essays, either of a particular scene or of a character, students can search their experiences or imaginations:

> outdoors--woods, seashore, mountains, fields, city
>   streets, parks
> indoors--dorm rooms, crowded auditoriums, laundromats
> scenes--family gatherings, holiday events, parties,
>   football games, funerals, accidents, a snowy morning
> people--parents, grandparents, uncles, aunts, neigh-
>   bors, childhood friends, people observed in a library
>   or a public place, cartoon characters like Snoopy,
>   roommates, teachers, unpleasant people

For expository essays, students can consider subjects like these:

> hobbies, jobs, games, investments, campus concerns,
> fields of study, recent scientific discoveries,
> computers, places to visit, ways to save money, ways
> to travel, parties, fishing and hunting, gardening,

study habits, repairing a car, sailing or canoeing, hospitals, stereo equipment, magazines, high school

For persuasive essays, students can consider subjects like these:

campus issues, local politics, environmental concerns such as a bottle bill or toxic waste disposal, automobile safety, government regulation of industry, drunken-driving laws, cost of medical care, regulation of new drugs, costs of education, specialized education vs. liberal arts education, rights of minorities and women, gun control, divorce and child raising, marriage, unions and corporations, school prayer, public and private schools, proposals to improve campus or local services, ways to deal with a health problem or a social problem, ways to improve an organization or institution

5. Limiting and Probing Topics. (a) Give students a list of general subjects—music, sports, guns, the environment—and ask them to explore each one, looking for limited aspects that might make good topics for essays. Class discussion can focus on how to limit the topics and indicate how an audience might respond to them. (b) Have students probe general subjects using the questions presented in Chapters 1 and 3 (pp. 9-12 and 83-90) as ways to develop essays and paragraphs: What is it? What are its parts? What are its causes or effects? And so on. These questions direct attention to different aspects of a subject and at the same time suggest ways of developing it and organizing an essay.

6. Grouping Ideas. If you ask students to jot down ideas (and facts) about a subject, they can often limit the topic and start to organize an essay by first circling those ideas that seem most interesting and closely related and then drawing lines to indicate relationships among the ideas. If the central and subordinate ideas are then arranged in subject trees that reflect logical relationships, they can suggest a pattern of organization for the essay.

7. Developing and Revising the Thesis. (a) Copy effective thesis statements from student papers to use in class discussion. They will provide positive models and may suggest topics for future essays. You can vary this exercise by copying ineffective statements and discussing word-by-word how they can be improved. (b) Write interesting

topics on the board, perhaps drawn from student essays, and
ask the class to come up with several different thesis
statements for the topics. (c) Ask students to read an
essay and then state its thesis in their own words. Next
have them look for a thesis statement in the essay. If the
essay has an explicit thesis statement, ask the students if
they consider it effective or if the thesis statements they
have arrived at would be more effective. If the thesis is
implicit, ask if the essay would benefit from an explicit
thesis statement. (d) Ask a student to read his or her
paper aloud in class, deliberately leaving out the thesis
statement. Ask the class to supply a thesis for the essay.
If the student's thesis and the class's match, fine. If
they do not, the thesis the student has chosen may be
inappropriate for the paper, and the class can discuss
possible changes.

       8. <u>Oral Progress Reports</u>. Have students report orally
to the class on topics and thesis statements for an upcoming
paper. Oral presentation forces students to focus their
ideas and adopt a stance. As they speak to the class, moreover, students may sense difficulties with the topic or
thesis. Comments from classmates can help identify
strengths and weaknesses and suggest an appropriate tone for
the essay.

       9. <u>Purpose Outlines</u>. Some students have trouble main-
taining unity of purpose and coherent organization in an
essay even after they have outlined it because the outline
describes the content of the essay but does not indicate the
function of each part. To help students overcome this problem, ask them to add a statement of purpose to each major
section of their outlines and to indicate how the section
will carry out the purposes of the paper. The following is
an example of such a statement:

> In this section I plan to explain how much money
> industries lose by failing to treat industrial
> waste to recover precious or expensive metals like
> chromium, gold, silver, and platinum. This will be the
> second of the three little-known costs of pollution
> that my thesis statement promises the paper will
> discuss.

Statements of purpose can alert students to potential
problems in the organization or unity of an essay, and they
provide instructors with a quick way to spot the problems.
Some instructors even ask students to submit "purpose
outlines" in place of formal outlines:

In this section of the paper I plan to show that there
is a real need for this university to provide more
funds for the library.
To support my point, I plan to explore three
three serious effects of underfunding--lack of
basic reference materials, lack of staff to
shelve books properly and check for missing
volumes, and poor maintenance of the library
building.

10. Audience Inventory. Ask students to make a list
of the kinds of people who might be interested in the
sujects of their essays. (In theory such a list might be
very long. In practice, students soon run out of ideas, but
not until they have begun to visualize the audience for
their essay.) To extend the exercise, ask students what part
of the potential audience they would most like to address or
what kinds of people would be most interested in a particular topic. Then ask them to list what the restricted
audience probably already knows about the topic and what it
needs to know, or what its attitudes are and what kinds of
arguments will be needed to change them.

11. Overcoming Writing Blocks. Many students have a
hard time writing first drafts because they try to get
everything right the first time. They end up writing sentences and then crossing out what they have written so often
that they have no time left to revise their thoughts in a
second draft. Sometimes the pressure of perfection is so
great the students become blocked writers, unable to finish
even a single draft before the deadline. Here are three
ways to help students get started: (a) Show them copies of
your own first and final drafts to indicate that you were
not afraid to make mistakes in the first draft because you
had a chance to correct them in the later drafts. (b) Give
students a time limit for the first draft, perhaps an hour
and a half or two hours, depending on the length of the
assignment. Require them to hand in the draft with the
final paper so you can see how they went about the job of
writing. (c) Have students start writing in class where you
can encourage them to get ideas down on paper before they
try to perfect the wording. (d) Require students to spend
some time either jotting down ideas and phrases or freewriting so they will be loosened up before they tackle the
first draft.

12. <u>Revising</u>. Chapter 2 of the <u>Handbook</u> already says a good deal about revising. Here are a few more activities that can help students revise effectively. (a) After students have written an initial draft, ask them to complete a brief version of the audience inventory (number 10 above) to help guide the choices they make during revision. (b) For narrative writing, ask students to circle every use of "He said that" and "She thought that" or similar phrases indicating indirect discourse. Then ask them to consider replacing the indirect discourse with dialogue and direct quotations in order to make the writing more vivid and realistic. (c) For narrative and descriptive writing, ask students to check how many of the senses they have drawn on; then ask them to consider making use of the other senses. (d) For argumentative essays, have students list all the arguments they could use but have not yet included in the paper. (e) For argumentative essays, ask students to summarize their theses and supporting arguments for the class and ask the class to suggest more supporting arguments and to come up with opposing arguments the writer might consider during revision. (f) For expository essays, ask students to answer these questions: What five things do you know about this topic that you have not included in the draft? Which could you put into your essay without harming its unity or coherence?

Chapter 3 "Composing Good Paragraphs"

The many similarities between expository (and argumentative) paragraphs and the essay as a whole make studying and practicing such paragraphs a good way for many students to develop their writing skills. All the basic features of expository and argumentative writing appear also in most individual paragraphs—generalizations supported by details, examples, reasons, or other kinds of specific information. The pattern of the typical paragraph, consisting of the statement of a topic or opinion followed by concrete comment on it, illustrates an essential essay pattern within a length and degree of complexity that students can manage. Moreover, just as the sentences in a paragraph must be related in ways that are immediately clear to a reader, so the paragraphs within an essay must move clearly from one to another. Thus by examining and constructing well-made paragraphs, students can become more confident and accomplished in managing multiparagraph papers. This, at least, is the assumption behind Chapter 3. Of course, the paragraphs in professional writing do not all conform in length, structure, or purpose to the models provided in the chapter.

Paragraphs in narrative and descriptive writing, dialogue paragraphs, introductory and concluding paragraphs, and paragraphs for emphasis or transition all frequently differ in some way from the standard pattern, differences noted and discussed in the chapter. Nonetheless, helping students master the so-called standard paragraph can be a good way to help them learn better.

The first main section of Chapter 3 (section 3a) addresses the need for a paragraph to focus on a topic and to make the focus clear to the reader through an explicit statement in the form of a topic sentence. This section introduces the basic form of the expository paragraph—topic sentence, optional sentence of clarification or limitation, illustrations and details—and indicates how this pattern can be varied to suit a writer's purpose. The concept of a clearly stated and variously placed topic sentence that controls the shape of the whole paragraph is, of course, an oversimplification. But it appears to help students a great deal to think of the paragraph as a unit dominated and controlled by an expressly stated generalization. Students can see the topic sentence as a commitment they make to the reader, with the rest of the paragraph following through on the commitment. The obvious parallel between the paragraph's topic sentence and the essay's thesis statement is also helpful to many students. Finally, of course, stating a central point in a single sentence and marshaling support for it enables students to see more clearly what is required for unity. The exercises for this section ask students to identify the parts and pattern of unified paragraphs, to revise a paragraph, to build a paragraph by combining and revising kernel sentences, and to write their own paragraphs by developing a given topic sentence. In this way students come to know not only the features of a finished, unified paragraph, but also the writing and revising process necessary to arrive at such a paragraph.

The second main section of the chapter (3b) deals with paragraph coherence, addressing it from the reader's perspective as well as the writer's. Students are shown how the devices they use to achieve paragraph coherence help readers to follow the arguments or information being presented. The section emphasizes the need to maintain a clear organizational pattern as one of the principal ways to ensure coherence. It also presents examples of basic patterns of organization, for students who have difficulty organizing their own writing can usually see the pattern of organization in a well-made paragraph. Following the discussion of patterns, the section takes up and illustrates other methods of achieving coherence: parallelism; careful use of pronouns; consistency in person, tense, and number;

repetition of words; and transitional expressions. Analysis of paragraphs can help students understand these explicit and implicit means by which individual sentences are held together so the reader follows effortlessly the flow of ideas and information. As in the preceding section, the exercises move from analysis to revision to production. They give students a chance to identify patterns in model paragraphs, revise scrambled paragraphs, build paragraphs from kernel sentences, and write paragraphs based on given topic sentences.

The third section (3c) looks at some ways to convey the central idea of a paragraph fully and convincingly to the reader. Developing paragraphs and essays fully is often a difficult job for students. One of the important differences between casual conversation and formal writing is the degree to which ideas must be concretely developed in writing. Because students are more experienced in conversation than in writing, they find generalizations much easier to come by than the details, examples, and reasons to support them, and most students have difficulty developing ideas. All of us must grapple with the student essay or single paragraph that is largely a succession of generalizations without support or explanation. Part of the solution to such problem paragraphs is to make students aware of readers as a special kind of audience for ideas. Another part is to make them aware of different strategies for developing paragraphs or essays.

The ways to develop ideas are infinite, of course, but this section focuses on a limited number. The initial emphasis falls on the use of details, examples, and reasons, which are essential to any more specific method of development. Then follow the standard methods or patterns of development, each introduced by questions students can ask about an idea, event, or object to uncover concrete information useful for developing a paragraph. You may wish to spend some time in class working with sample topics to show how the methods of development can be used to probe a topic and how the questions reveal different aspects of a topic. This discussion may help students see how the process of development can be an act of discovery. You will probably want to stress, however, that the methods of development covered in the Handbook are not the only ones writers can use and that most paragraphs use more than a single method. The exercises for this section range from analyzing paragraphs to producing them and encourage students to treat the methods of development as different ways to view a topic.

The next section (3d) deals with the special problems of introductory and concluding paragraphs, the occasional usefulness of transitional paragraphs, and the conventions

of paragraphing in dialogue. The emphasis you give to
introductory and concluding paragraphs may vary with the
experience of your students. For some writers writing a
straightforward introductory paragraph that simply sets the
stage for the essay and presents a thesis statement will be
an accomplishment. Others will benefit from experimenting
with some of the variations illustrated. Because concluding
paragraphs often present a special problem, you may wish to
highlight the common inept endings that trap students and to
suggest satisfactory alternatives.

The last section (3e) brings together the principles
covered in the preceding sections in an extended discussion
of a model essay. The model essay shows how effective
writing makes use of paragraphs following various methods
and weaves them into a coherent, unified whole. This section can be the basis for discussion in class of student
papers, or it can be a good bridge to a treatment of the
whole essay. You may wish to use Exercise 4 in Chapter 2,
which asks students to analyze student essays, and Exercise
20 in Chapter 3, which provides paragraphs for analysis.

Activities and Assignments

1. Creating Unified Paragraphs. Give the class five
topic sentences on different subjects and ask each student
to choose one and write a unified paragraph based on it.
Then ask students to read their paragraphs aloud and have
the class check for unity and compare methods of development.

2. Coloring Paragraphs. Bring in copies of sample
paragraphs and felt-tipped pens or pencils in three colors.
Split the class into groups and ask each group to underline
topic sentences in one color, sentences of limitation in
another, and examples and details in the third. Students
should then be able to identify the shape of each paragraph
and to understand how the parts fit together to form a
unified whole.

3. Paragraph Patterns I. Give students a topic sentence and a set of assertions, facts, and details in unde-
veloped form. Tell them to use the material to write a
coherent paragraph following one of the patterns described
in the Handbook: spatial, chronological, general-to-spe-
cific, specific-to-general, less dramatic-to-more dramatic.
Students can manipulate the material in any way they wish to
achieve an effect that is appropriate to the pattern. You

may also want to ask for several paragraphs, each using the same content but with a different pattern.

4. <u>Paragraph Patterns II</u>. As a quiz or in-class exercise, ask students to write a paragraph following one of the basic patterns of organization discussed in 3b-1. Leave the subject and content of the paragraph up to the individual student. If they wish, students may make up information, as long as they keep it plausible.

5. <u>Paragraph Scrambles</u>. (a) Take a good paragraph, by either a student or a professional, and rearrange the sentences. Then ask students to unscramble the sentences and make a clear, coherent paragraph. This exercise will make students aware of the flow of a coherent paragraph and alert them to the number of examples and details found in a well-developed paragraph. (b) Choose a paragraph that lacks coherence and rearrange the sentences. Tell students to unscramble the sentences to form a coherent paragraph. Indicate that they are free to add any transitions, sentences, illustrations, or details they feel are necessary to make the paragraph both coherent and well developed. Students will spot quickly any coherence problems in the original paragraph, and unless the topic of the paragraph is quite unusual, they will be able to add any necessary content.

6. <u>Developing Paragraphs</u>. Take underdeveloped paragraphs on subjects likely to be familiar to students and ask them to develop the paragraphs fully by drawing on their own knowledge. Student paragraphs often provide good material for this exercise.

7. <u>Imitating Paragraphs</u>. Choose a successful paragraph with a clear pattern, student or professional, and discuss it in class. Then ask students to write paragraphs imitating the pattern of the model paragraph but with different content.

8. <u>Imitating Openings and Closings</u>. When experienced writers have trouble beginning or ending essays, they usually turn to strategies that have been successful on other occasions. To help student writers develop similar resources, distribute opening and closing paragraphs with particularly effective strategies and ask students to write their own paragraphs using the same strategies but with different content.

9. <u>Magazine Models</u>. Magazines like <u>Time</u>, <u>Glamour</u>, <u>Outdoor Life</u>, and <u>Self</u> contain a variety of informative articles. The authors of these articles and students writing expository essays face a similar problem--how to get readers interested enough to keep reading. Have students collect effective openings and bring them to class for discussion. Students can also comb editorials and magazine articles for openings of argumentative essays.

10. <u>Combining for Emphasis</u>. Put together a group of sentences or bits of information about a topic, perhaps drawing the material from an essay in a reader or a magazine article. Ask students to combine the material into a paragraph with a distinct point of view. You might, for example, provide information about a recent controversial incident and ask for a paragraph that emphasizes one perspective toward the incident.

Chapter 4 "Convincing a Reader"

Chapter 4 is an extension of the discussion of audience in the first chapter. Instead of being isolated from concerns of audience, as is frequently the case, the discussion of logic and logical fallacies in student and professional writing comes in a context that relates more fundamentally to problems students are likely to encounter in their writing. The first three sections of the chapter deal with moderate tone; clearly defined terms; distinctions among fact, judgment or opinion, and prejudice; and adequate evidence for assertions. Included are brief discussions of begging and ignoring the question, common tactics by which writers evade the central question they purport to discuss. Also included in the chapter is an important positive treatment of kinds of evidence that provide reliable support for assertions. The fourth section of the chapter offers simplified explanations of inductive and deductive reasoning and explains through concrete examples several of the most common fallacies that interfere with inductive reasoning. The exercises for the chapter reinforce all its features.

Activities and Assignments

1. Analyzing Issues. Have students discuss a campus
issue like residential policies, parking arrangements,
library or computer services, trying to identify the
assertions and supporting evidence on each side of the
argument. List the assertions and evidence on the board so
students can distinguish fact from opinion and identify
terms that need definition. If students know enough about
issues of public policy such as gun control, capital
punishment, or a bottle bill, these topics can be used for
discussion.

2. Examining Ads. Distribute ads from a magazine or
newspaper and ask students to identify any attempts to avoid
the question or any logical fallacies in the ads.

3. Evidence in Editorials. Distribute copies of
newpaper editorials and ask students to evaluate the
evidence the editorials contain for accuracy, relevance,
representativeness, and adequacy.

Part II GRAMMATICAL SENTENCES

Chapter 5   "Understanding Sentence Grammar"

Chapter 5 presents a brief descriptive grammar that can
serve not only as a reference for explanations of basic
grammatical terms but also as a guide to how English sentences are constructed. Rather than compartmentalizing
grammar into eight parts of speech, kinds of phrases and
clauses, and kinds of sentences, Chapter 5 builds cumula-
tively from the simplest sentence to increasingly complex
expansions. Because of this approach and because of the
many sentence-combining and sentence-modeling exercises it
contains, Chapter 5 can be useful for a wide range of
students, from remedial to advanced. Students whose writing
displays fundamental problems with sentences will benefit
from its clear treatment of sentence parts and structure and
from the exercises that require manipulation of sentence
elements. Students who have mastered basic sentence
strategies will be able to develop a wide range of options
for expression through sentence-combining exercises that
introduce elements like verbal phrases, absolute phrases,
and appositives.
    The chapter begins (5a) with the basic subject-
predicate sentence composed only of nouns, their substitute

pronouns, and verbs; it moves to predicates formed from simple verb-noun combinations. The introduction of five basic sentence patterns at this point allows teachers to require students to create sentences following the patterns as well as to identify the elements of sample sentences.

The basic modifying words, adjectives and adverbs, are taken up next (5b) as the most elementary means of expanding the simple subject-predicate sentence. At this point the ability of some verb forms and nouns to modify is introduced briefly. The patterning and combining exercises in this section give students a chance to practice adding modifiers to sentences and to see the effect modifiers have on both the impact and the meaning of sentences. Even at this basic level the exercises can provide a focus for discussion of the effects of different sentence strategies.

The third section of the chapter (5c) further expands the basic sentence with syntactic word groups: prepositional, verbal, and absolute phrases; subordinate clauses; and appositives. It is here, in the context of their use, that prepositions and subordinating conjunctions come up. The emphasis throughout this section is on how these word groups actually perform, within varying constraints, the same functions as the four basic word classes of the language. Further, both the text and the˙ accompanying exercises encourage students to work with these word groups to achieve greater flexibility and precision in their own sentences, not merely to learn grammatical terms for the sake of identification. The elements discussed in this and following sections are the building blocks of complex, effective sentences. The sentence-combining exercises following each discussion provide students with an opportunity to use the word groups in writing and can be a good classroom activity. (For a fuller treatment of the use of such exercises, see "Sentence Combining with The Little, Brown Handbook" in Chapter 1 of this Manual.)

The fourth section of the chapter (5d) describes the compounding of words, phrases, and clauses and introduces coordinating and correlative conjunctions and conjunctive adverbs as words that link elements in compound structures. The explanations emphasize how compounding often achieves economy in sentences. The examples and exercises stress the usefulness of compounding and give students a chance to practice various options in their writing. Though the features and relationships covered in this section may seem a bit basic to some students, an understanding of them is essential to proper punctuation. Many punctuation errors, both basic and sophisticated, are the result of a misunderstanding of sentence structure. Such errors include run-ons, misuse of the semicolon, commas that separate elements in a compound subject or predicate, and sentence fragments.

The last two brief sections of the chapter (5e and 5f) describe alterations in the basic subject-predicate pattern (questions, commands, passive sentences, and postponed subjects) and the conventional classification of sentences according to their clause structure. An understanding of these various sentence strategies is necessary if students are to benefit from the stylistic options presented in Part IV, "Effective Sentences."

Chapter 5 uses almost entirely traditional terminology because such terminology, despite its weaknesses, is still the most widely used and most likely to be familiar to students and instructors. The overall description largely reflects a structural view of English grammar. It is as simple as possible while still including all the word classes and syntactic structures needed by the student to understand the twenty successive chapters on sentences and punctuation.

You may wish to emphasize or de-emphasize Chapter 5, depending in part on the preparation of your students and on how much you think an understanding of grammar can con-tribute to their writing. As may be obvious, this chapter of the Handbook was prepared in the belief that a clear understanding of the essential structure of English sen-tences and of the uses of syntactic groups and compound structures can help many students not only punctuate correctly but also gain greater control of subordination and emphasis within their sentences. This process will take place only if students get a chance to put knowledge into action through exercises that ask them to manipulate and create sentences. In this regard, we now know that sen-tence-combining activities such as those in Chapter 5 can build confidence and develop the ability to use mature, flexible sentence strategies. These sentence-combining exercises can be combined with those in other chapters of the text to create a program of sentence combining designed to complement instruction in essay and paragraph writing.

Activities and Assignments

Since Chapter 5 contains numerous exercises, most instructors will find no need for supplemental assignments. For those instructors who wish to vary their use of class time, however, the following activities may prove useful or may suggest other activities:

1. <u>Dictation</u>. Read the words in the list below or a
similar one to the class and then go through the list again,
giving students a minute or two to write sentences using the
words in as many different roles (parts of speech) as they
can. The word <u>good</u>, for example, can be an adjective or a
noun.

well	post	while
set	bill	bit
that	needle	turn

2. <u>Create Your Own</u>. Split the class into groups. Ask
each group to create its own set of sentence-combining exercises following the pattern of the exercises in the
<u>Handbook</u>. Then ask the groups to trade exercises, work on
them, and return them to the authors with both positive
comments and criticisms.

3. <u>Using the Reader</u>. Students can analyze passages
from an essay in a reader, looking for verbal phrases,
passive sentences, compound and complex sentences, or any
other features you feel contribute to the effect of the
essay and should be part of the students' prose style.

Chapters 6 to 9   "Case of Nouns and Pronouns"; "Verb Forms,
    Tense, Mood, and Voice"; "Agreement"; "Adjectives and
    Adverbs"

As the titles of these successive chapters indicate,
they address problems of grammar related to the forms of
nouns, pronouns, and verbs and the distinctions made between
adjective and adverb forms. These, of course, are the problems deriving from the few inflections still used as grammatical devices in English. Most violations of inflection
seldom interfere seriously with our understanding of a sentence because other, stronger grammatical signals are almost
always present. Yet the errors can be irritating, sometimes
even a bit confusing; they require more effort from readers
and some people regard them as marks of a lack of writing
(or language) ability or as signs of carelessness. Thus the
forms remain important in standard written English and are
usually observed in careful speech. Many of them constitute
serious problems for students, particularly those who have
had limited contact with standard English.
    Chapters 6 to 9 address problematic constructions, with
emphasis on those proved by experience to be especially
troublesome for students: pronoun form in a compound ob-
ject; <u>who</u> versus <u>whom</u>; irregular verb forms; the −<u>s</u> and −<u>ed</u>

inflections of verbs; and the like. The text notes when inflectional distinctions are eroding in the speech of even educated speakers or when usage fluctuates in the written language. However, it also consistently recommends that students observe the more conservative usage, a practice which is more likely to spare them unnecessary criticism.

Each of the four chapters includes a brief, simple explanation of a general problem and then, in several subsections, treats related problems likely to cause difficulty. Throughout these chapters and in successive ones dealing with clear sentences, punctuation, and mechanics, the rules are stated positively rather than negatively whenever possible. If students can see the description of conventional usage as a guide to dealing with problems—rather than as a set of red-light warnings about what they must not do—they may acquire a more constructive attitude toward their own writing. Then, after their composition course, students may continue to turn to the Handbook and more specialized references for guidance, just as we do.

Exercises appear quite frequently throughout these chapters. Wherever practicable, the exercises ask students to do more than choose between a right and a wrong form. Instead, to give students experience that they can apply more directly to their own sentences, the exercises ask students to revise errors after recognizing them or to produce error-free sentences by a variety of means including sentence combining and changing the tense of the verb or the number of the subject.

Chapter 6 "Case of Nouns and Pronouns"

This chapter opens with a review of the different functions a pronoun can perform, functions that determine the form, or case, of the pronoun. In addition to the familiar list of forms of the personal pronouns, the chapter provides sentences illustrating the wide variety of uses for pronouns. Following this are brief discussions of the proper case for pronouns in contexts that usually cause difficulty for student writers, including compound subjects and objects, appositives, comparisons using than or as, possessive case with gerunds, and the different uses of who and whom. The exercises ask students to select the appropriate forms of pronouns in the troublesome contexts treated in the discussion, and a set of sentence-combining exercises focuses on who and whom in relative clauses.

Activities and Assignments

 1. The Diagram. Students may be tempted to skim over the list of the forms of the personal pronouns at the beginning of the chapter. Get them to pay attention by asking them to fill the whole chart out in class--without looking at the text. The act of remembering the forms or figuring them out will be more valuable than listening to an explanation. Students who have trouble filling out the list probably need to spend time reviewing the chapter.

 2. Make Up Your Own Test. Give students time in class to write out five to ten sentences in quiz form. The easiest way for students to do this is to pattern their questions after the exercises and sample sentences in the Handbook:

> Most of (we, us) college students realize that finding a good job isn't easy.
> There is a five-hundred-dollar reward for (whomever, whoever) finds the missing stock certificates.

Students can make use of the Handbook in preparing the questions, and as long as they know that one of the possible answers they have provided must be right, students need not be sure which one it is. When the tests are completed, students should exchange them and fill them out. Correcting is best done in small groups so students can help one another or turn to the instructor to settle disputes and provide answers to the toughest questions.

 3. Back to Nouns. Distribute a paragraph taken from a magazine article, an essay in a reader, or a student paper. Ask students to rewrite it, substituting the appropriate noun for each pronoun. This will help students understand the role of pronouns and see the relationship between the case of a pronoun and the function of the noun it stands for.

Chapter 7 "Verb Forms, Tense, Mood, and Voice"

 Verb tense can cause trouble for students in three ways: They may choose the wrong form (inflection) of a verb, they may choose the wrong tense, or they may shift tenses improperly. For students who have trouble with verb forms, particularly the -s and -ed inflections and irregular verbs, the chapter provides thorough explanations, a list of the principal parts of frequently used verbs, and exercises.

The chapter also reviews verb tense, placing special emphasis on the different uses of the present and perfect tenses. Sequence of tenses and use (or misuse) of the passive voice can become important as students begin to write ambitious narratives and expository or argumentative essays. The chapter reviews proper sequence of tenses and draws a careful distinction between proper and improper uses of the passive voice.

Activities and Assignments

1. Verb Tense and Sequence--Pictures and Events. Show students a picture containing a scene that suggests some preceding events as well as some that might follow. Ask them to write a brief narrative describing the sequence of events and making use of proper verb forms and the correct sequence of tenses.

2. Creating a Story. Write on the board a sentence containing one or more characters and an action. Here are some examples:

As he rounded the corner, John heard a loud noise, somewhere between a crash and a bang.
As he came into the classroom, Jim noticed that Carolyn was already there reviewing her notes.

Ask students to write a paragraph-length story (seven to eight sentences) beginning with the sentence you have given them, maintaining a correct sequence of tenses, containing proper verb forms, and using a variety of action verbs.

3. Discussion Story. Put a lead sentence (as in number 2) on the board, and ask the class as a whole to decide on the events that follow it. Summarize the events briefly, then ask students to write out the story, making it as vivid as possible. This will provide both oral and written practice with verb tense and sequence.

4. Passive Sentences--Count the Words. Write on the board a number of sentences in the active voice ranging from simple sentences to relatively complex ones. Ask students to change the sentences into the passive voice and then to count the number of words in each version. Finally, ask students to read some of the passive sentences aloud and comment on their effectiveness. This exercise will allow you to check students' understanding of the passive voice and at the same time demonstrate its wordiness.

   5. <u>Passive Sentences--Finding Passages.</u> Have students
locate passive sentences in an essay from a reader or a similar source. Ask them to decide if the passive provides
emphasis appropriate for the essay or if the active voice
would be better.

Chapter 8 "Agreement"

   Some students may have difficulty with basic subject-
verb agreement, particularly with the -s or -es endings that
mark plural nouns and singular verbs in standard English.
But almost all students encounter problems with subject-verb
or pronoun-antecedent agreement when they begin writing the
complicated, information-filled sentences characteristic of
essays in college composition courses. Chapter 8 pays
special attention to the sentence structures that make it
difficult for student writers to determine the correct
relationship in number between subjects and verbs or pronouns and antecedents. These structures include compound
subjects, collective nouns, relative and indefinite pronouns, phrases like "one of the," and widely separated
subjects and verbs. Rather than treating agreement problems
as errors resulting from ignorance, the chapter treats them
for the most part as areas requiring special attention, a
point of view with which most instructors are likely to
agree because even experienced writers sometimes have to
turn to a handbook for help with agreement.
   The chapter's treatment of pronoun-antecedent agreement
takes special note of problems with indefinite pronouns
caused by recent changes in the language. In speech, even
some educated speakers treat indefinite pronouns like
<u>anybody</u> and <u>everyone</u> as plural: "Everybody ought to pay
attention to their own business." This change may in part
reflect a desire to avoid the generic <u>he</u>, a form of usage
many people regard as sexist. While the chapter makes clear
the need to treat <u>everybody</u>, <u>someone</u>, and the like as singular, at least in the more conservative written medium, it
also presents alternative strategies to avoid sexist
language.
   The exercises for the chapter ask students to recognize
and revise agreement errors in both sentences and a longer
passage and to change verbs and pronouns as needed when
changing the number of the subject.

Activities and Assignments

1. <u>Are Everyone Ready?</u> Though many students will not, at first, hear anything wrong with sentences like "Everyone ought to pay attention to their own business," a pattern that is gaining some acceptance in speech, almost all will find sentences like these unacceptable: "Are everyone ready for lunch?" "Do everybody have enough money to buy tickets for the rides?" Anyone who finds the latter sentences acceptable is probably having trouble recognizing the singular and plural forms of verbs. Sample sentences can, therefore, help you identify the real source of a student's agreement problems.

2. <u>Widely Separated Subjects and Verbs</u>. Using the explanations and examples in the <u>Handbook</u> as a guide, ask your students to identify the sentence strategies that often result in widely separated subjects and verbs. Then ask the students to write sentences using the strategies and containing proper subject-verb agreement. (This exercise can also be used with compound subjects, collective nouns, inverted word order, or other strategies that frequently lead to agreement problems.)

3. <u>Using Magazines or a Reader</u>. Using essays from a reader or magazine articles, have students look for sentence structures often associated with agreement problems. Show students how important these structures are for expository prose and indicate how important it that they master the structures without creating agreement problems.

Chapter 9 "Adjectives and Adverbs"

Many readers view the misuse of adjectives and adverbs as a sign of ignorance and carelessness. Students should be alerted to the potential effect of errors and urged to pay attention to the advice in the text. This chapter, however, takes a positive approach, showing students the correct way to use adjectives and adverbs rather than emphasizing the don'ts. The exercises in the chapter ask students not only to recognize errors but also to revise sentences to make sure adjectives and adverbs are used appropriately.

Activities and Assignments

1. <u>Rewrite to Cause Error</u>. Take an acceptable passage from a student paper, an essay in a reader, or a magazine article and rewrite it to introduce errors in the use of

adjectives and adverbs. Distribute the passage to students, ask them to correct it, and then distribute the original and ask them to comment on any differences between their corrections and the original version.

2. Homemade Quizzes. Ask students to follow the pattern of the sample sentences and exercises in the chapter and make up sentences containing common errors in the use of adjectives and adverbs. The uses of well and good, bad and badly are good starters. Collect the papers and distribute them as quizzes during the next class. Correct them in small groups.

Part III CLEAR SENTENCES

Chapters 10 to 15 treat common problems that can interfere with the meaning of sentences and damage a reader's view of the writer's competence. With the exception of sentence fragments, comma splices, and run-on (fused) sentences, the matters treated in these chapters are as much grammatical problems as those, like agreement, that derive from inflections in the language. As noted in the preceding section, however, errors involving inflectional forms may distract readers but rarely influence their ability to understand a writer's meaning. In contrast, misplaced modifiers, confused pronoun reference, shifts in structure, and mixed or incomplete constructions can easily confuse or mislead readers about the writer's intentions. And failures to mark clearly the boundaries of sentences (comma splices, run-ons, and fragments), while of a different order, often have the same effect. In short, failure to control the matters discussed in Chapters 10 to 15 can impair a writer's ability to communicate meaning clearly to his or her audience.

Chapters 10 and 11 "Sentence Fragments"; "Comma Splices and Run-on Sentences"

Chapters 10 and 11 deal with sentence fragments and with comma splices and run-on (fused) sentences. From one perspective, these are punctuation problems, not grammatical ones, because in most cases they stem from students' lack of familiarity with the conventions of punctuation. Yet they are placed here among grammatical problems because in some cases they may be caused by a failure to recognize sentence boundaries and because, whatever the cause, students who repeatedly use sentence fragments or run-on sentences can revise them only by understanding the basic grammatical requirements for a complete sentence.

Chapter 10 opens with a positive approach by showing students how to determine whether a word group is a complete sentence or a fragment. It follows with advice about avoiding a common error that leads to sentence fragments: the punctuation of a sentence part--subordinate clause, verbal phrase, prepositional phrase, appositive, or part of a compound predicate--as a complete sentence. Exercises for the chapter ask students to identify and rewrite fragments and to split sentences in two without creating fragments. Chapter 11 gives advice for recognizing and correcting comma splices and run-ons. Correction of these errors may involve strategies that students should employ more frequently in their sentences, particularly subordination and use of the semicolon. To encourage variety in sentence structure along with the avoidance of error, exercises for the chapter ask students to combine sentences following different strategies as well as to recognize and revise run-ons and comma splices.

Both of the chapters depart in some ways from the general inclination to treat matters positively and instead provide a series of don'ts. Of course, accomplished writers often use sentence fragments effectively and separate certain kinds of main clauses only with a comma; and these exceptions are acknowledged briefly. But conventionally unacceptable fragments, comma splices, and run-on sentences are so likely to impress readers as incompetent that it seems sensible to advise students very strongly against using the structures at all--at least until they can manage standard, complete sentences whose clauses are separated strictly according to convention. If your students can distinguish appropriate from inappropriate or unconventional uses of fragments and splices, you can easily temper the Handbook's advice, and you will doubtless want to do so.

Activities and Assignments

1. Fragments, Comma Splices, and Run-ons in Context. Identifying sentence problems in the context of an essay can be more challenging and rewarding than working with single-sentence examples. The content and flow of an essay can draw attention away from punctuation and sentence structure, making it hard to identify errors but also providing an experience similar to that of proofreading. Revise part of a professional essay to introduce errors or find an error-filled student essay. Distribute the essay to the class and ask students to locate and revise the errors.

2. Advertising. Advertisements and public announcements frequently contain fragments, run-ons, and comma splices. In fact, some people speculate that this may be one source of problems in student writing. Collect examples from magazine ads, junk mail, signs, and similar places and ask students to spot and correct the errors. Here are two examples, the first from an advertisement, the second from a hotel's restaurant menu.

> Introducing the Satellite News Channel. The first all-live, all-news TV channel. News with no fillers. No reruns. No nonsense. No fat.
> SNC is live-action news, delivered fresh every 18 minutes. Powered by the world-wide resources of ABC Television and Group W Broadcasting. With the depth of 24 award-winning regional news teams. Available 24-hours a day. Seven days a week.

> PICNIC LUNCH AVAILABLE.
> Please give your order 1 hour in advance. Before 10:00 AM. Good Morning we hope you will have a pleasant day.

Some students may wish to argue that the fragments they find are used appropriately. The ensuing discussion is likely to be worthwhile.

3. Creating Problems. Ask students to write sample sentences containing run-ons, or comma splices, and fragments. Then have them exchange papers and check to see if the errors have been executed properly. This exercise will help students recognize run-ons, comma splices, and fragments. (It's much harder to create intentional errors, particularly sentence fragments, than most students will think.)

4. Newscasters. The breathless style of radio and television newscasts often includes fragments and groups of words that sound run-on. Ask students to write down examples from the evening news. Newspapers, especially tabloids, can be a good source, too.

Chapters 12 to 15   "Prounoun Reference"; "Shifts"; "Misplaced and Dangling Modifiers"; "Mixed and Incomplete Sentences"

These four chapters are likely to receive heavy use, particularly as students begin to write papers that are ambitious in style and content. Chapters 12 to 15 describe the need for clear reference of pronouns (12); the shifts in person, tense, voice, and mood that destroy consistency and either distract or confuse the reader (13); the problems of modifier position caused by the English sentence's heavy reliance on word order (14); and the problems of mixed sentences and incomplete constructions, including comparisons (15). Students vary widely, of course, in the extent to which they have trouble with these matters. Some problems --such as shifts between the second and third person and reference of pronouns--are troublesome simply because formal writing is so much more conservative than speech.

Chapter 12 "Pronoun Reference"

This chapter covers a number of reference problems particularly troublesome for students: unclear or ambiguous antecedents; indefinite use of it and they; and inappropriate use of who, which, and that. In each case, the discussion stresses the need for precision in reference as a way of ensuring that readers can follow the meaning of a passage. The examples and exercises in the text mostly show reference problems within sentences as a way of keeping the discussion as simple and accessible as possible, but the text points out that reference problems are just as likely to occur between sentences, a fact you may want to emphasize in class. Because strings of pronouns are an important device for creating coherence over long stretches of discourse, reference problems between, or among, sentences can cause considerable misunderstanding. Activities 2 and 3 below alert students to the role of reference in clusters of sentences and in paragraphs.

Activities and Assignments

1. Retrieving Sentences. Reverse the process of sentence combining by asking students to reconstruct (or retrieve) the shorter (kernel) sentences that lie behind a long sentence containing a reference error. You may wish to use sentences from the Handbook as a basis for the exercise. This activity will help students spot ambiguity or vague reference in the long sentence. After they have found the shorter sentences, ask students to recombine, this time avoiding the reference problem.

Original sentence: After the van hit John's car, its engine stopped running and its radiator started

leaking.
Kernels: The van hit John's car. The van's engine
stopped running. The van's radiator started leaking.
Recombined sentence: After the van hit John's car, the
van's engine stopped running and its radiator started
leaking.

2. <u>Correcting a Narrative</u>. Find or write a brief
narrative containing several events and more than one character. Introduce enough reference problems so that it is
difficult for readers to unravel the events. If you wish,
include dialogue in the narrative in such a way that the
reference problems make it hard to identify the speakers.
(Using "He said" as a tag when there are two men in the
narrative is one possibility.) Ask students to rewrite the
narrative to remove vague and ambiguous reference.

3. <u>It, They, and Which</u>. Make a copy of a student paper
that uses <u>it</u>, <u>they</u>, <u>which</u>, and other pronouns in sentences
without supplying clear antecedents in preceding sentences.
Ask students to correct the reference problems and discuss
with them how a string of pronouns can be used properly to
bring coherence to writing.

Chapter 13 "Shifts"

Shifts in person and number, in tense and mood, in
subject and voice, or between direct and indirect quotation
can be irritating to readers and occasionally make it hard to
follow the meaning of a passage. Often, however, students
are not fully aware of the shifts or their effect on a
reader. This chapter describes in detail and illustrates the
various shifts so that students can learn to identify the
problems in their own writing. The exercises ask students to
revise sentences and a longer passage much as they will have
to revise their own work.

1. <u>Class Reading</u>. Use the passage below, or find or
write another that contains several different kinds of
shifts. Distribute copies to the class and read through it
with the students, asking them to identify the problems.
This will help make them aware of different kinds of shifts
as they appear in the context of an essay.

As soon as the avalanche was over, Jim pulls himself
out of the snowbank and yells, "Where's everybody?" and
were we still alive. As each of us in turn started
digging out, you could see the damage the huge wall of

snow had caused. The snow had destroyed the lodge and cars were swept away. . . .

2. Check Your Own. If shifts are a problem in the essays your class submits, go over the chapter in detail in class, and then ask students to go through their papers and circle each shift they find. This can be done on the day papers are to be handed in or with a set of graded papers on which you have not marked the shifts. This is also a good small-group exercise; students often do a very good job spotting shifts in someone else's writing.

Chapter 14 "Misplaced and Dangling Modifiers"

Misplaced and dangling modifiers often interest students because the faulty constructions can be amusing. To tie together all the different problems discussed in the chapter, however, you may want to point out that they all illustrate the importance of position and arrangement in sentences. Split constructions (14e and 14f) conveniently emphasize the need to keep the parts of related syntactic groups clearly unified. Yet both standard speech and formal writing provide frequent examples of freely placed limiting modifiers and of split infinitives. Part of our difficulty in teaching composition is in giving students effective advice about when freedom is constructive and when it is confusing. As in all such matters, the advice of the Handbook is largely conservative, so you may want to modify it.

Activities and Assignments

1. Sentence Combining. Exercise 6 in the Handbook (p. 246) requires students to combine pairs of sentences whose content and structure make them likely causes of misplaced or dangling modifiers. Extend this activity by having students create their own sentences that would be easy to miscombine. Choose the best pairs, copy them, and have the class do them for an exercise.

2. Moving Only. Ask students to create sentences whose meaning changes as a modifier like only moves from place to place:

> Only students were asked to bring gym shorts and running shoes.
> Students were only asked to bring gym shorts and running shoes.

Students were asked only to bring gym shorts and running shoes.

Students were asked to bring only gym shorts and running shoes.

3. The Media. Radio and television newscasts are rich sources of dangling and misplaced modifiers, perhaps because reporters have little time to pay attention to the structure of their sentences. Have students listen to newscasts and record errors; this will help them understand the perspective of a reader who comes across similar errors in an essay. Newspaper headlines, public announcements, and government documents are also rich sources; from time to time, magazine articles and paperback books appear with collections of particularly humorous errors. But students will be able to find many on their own by looking at the newspaper for headlines like "Young Man, 17, Slain by Road."

Chapter 15 "Mixed and Incomplete Sentences"

The first two sections of Chapter 15 deal with sentences whose subjects and predicates are incompatible. The tangled sentences in some student writing have more complex causes than this brief discussion of mixed sentences suggests. But the two most common problems do seem to be subjects and predicates that are incompatible in grammar (15a) and in meaning (15b). Section 15c deals with compound constructions that are grammatically or idiomatically incomplete. Ill-prepared students seem to encounter the problem less often than better-prepared students do, perhaps because only the latter use such constructions. On the other hand, incomplete comparisons (15d) are common, and you may wish to call particular attention to them. Section 15e, covering omission of needed words, is designed primarily as an aid to grading papers. Instructors who notice words missing in a student essay can call attention to the problem by using the number-and-letter code to refer students to this section.

Activities and Assignments

Because the mixed and incomplete sentences in student writing have complicated clauses and because the problems in each student's essay are likely to be quite different from those in other students' papers, most instructors choose simply to discuss the chapter and use some of the exercises rather than elaborate with classroom activities and assignments. In working with individual students, however, most instructors are able to devise activities that suit individual needs. Instructors who wish to alert students to the problems of incomplete compound constructions, incomplete comparisons, and omission of needed words can draw from a student paper or write a passage containing these problems and then ask students to proofread the passage and correct the errors.

PART IV EFFECTIVE SENTENCES

The four chapters in Part IV of the Handbook (Chapters 16 to 19) address primarily the rhetorical effectiveness of sentences rather than their grammatical "correctness." The matters covered in the chapters--subordination and coordination, parallelism, emphasis, and variety--are all important features of rhetorically effective and stylistically appropriate writing. Clearly, all these elements work together and are in many ways inseparable: Coordinate structures are almost necessarily parallel; and emphasis and variety cannot be achieved without confident control of coordination and subordination. Nonetheless, these concerns are treated in separate chapters on the assumption that students who are not well prepared can focus more easily on one at a time. Inevitably, there is redundancy among the chapters, and it is acknowledged not only in the textual explanations but also in cross-references. Thus, if you wish to emphasize the interrelations among these four chapters, you can easily do so.

These chapters, which deal mostly with matters of choice, not of necessity or convention, break away from the more prescriptive mode of the previous sentence chapters by phrasing headings descriptively rather than imperatively. And the chapters contain a variety of sentence-combining exercises designed to give students a chance to practice using the sentence strategies they have just read about. You may want to assign these chapters and their exercises as part of a unit on sentence style. Another approach is to assign a few exercises for each class as part of a program of sentence combining that runs for much of the semester. If you choose the latter approach, you may wish to supplement the chapters by making up sentence-combining exercises of your own, perhaps concentrating on paragraph-length activities.

A Guide to The Little, Brown Handbook

Chapter 16 "Using Coordination and Subordination"

The discussion in Chapter 16 emphasizes through explanations and examples how the writer can use subordination and coordination to distinguish central ideas and to clarify the relation of subordinated material to the central ideas. Section 16a first illustrates how coordination relates facts and ideas and then addresses the problems of faulty and excessive coordination. Section 16b follows a parallel pattern in its discussion of subordination, focusing on subordinate clauses. But since effective writing depends on the writer's ability to work with the whole range of subordinate structures, the uses of single words, appositives, and prepositional, verbal, and absolute phrases are also illustrated. The final section (16c) cautions briefly against the often unclear and misused connectors <u>like</u>, <u>while</u>, and <u>as</u>.

The exercises in this chapter ask students to revise sentences and longer passages and to combine sentences in ways that put into use the sentence strategies introduced in the chapter.

1. <u>Identifying</u>. Have students identify the connectors (subordinating and coordinating conjunctions) in several different essays: an essay from a reader, a news item in a newspaper, or a student essay. If the uses of subordination and coordination and the kinds of connectors differ in each kind of essay, ask students to explain why.

2. <u>Rewriting</u>. Give students a passage from a student or professional essay, and ask them to rewrite it following a specified strategy: adding subordination, using different subordinators, or adding coordination. This exercise can be extended by having students rewrite the passage to change its emphasis.

3. <u>Getting a New Look at Your Writing</u>. Give students a fresh look at their own writing by asking them to revise a portion of a graded essay following specific directions, such as, "Add subordination" or "Use more imaginative subordinating words."

4. <u>Reducing</u>. To help students practice subordination, give them a passage and ask them to reduce sentences to clauses and again, if possible, to words. After they have reduced the modifiers in these stages, ask them which version they find most effective.

Chapter 17 "Using Parallelism"

The treatment of parallelism in Chapter 17 is divided into two sections. Section 17a addresses the obligatory use of parallelism in coordinate constructions--those linked by coordinating conjunctions and correlative conjunctions, those in comparisons and contrasts, and those in lists, outlines, and the like. Section 17b examines how parallelism can be used within and among sentences to increase coherence, emphasize meaning, and heighten the effect. If your students are not well prepared, you will probably wish to emphasize the items in 17a. But students who have no problem maintaining obligatory parallelism can often profit by working more creatively with parallelism to tighten and clarify their writing. Exercise 3, a sentence-combining exercise, is designed to give students a chance to explore the options for expression that parallelism provides.

Activities and Assignments.

1. Sample Essays. Ask students to look for parallelism in essays from a reader or a similar source. This activity can help students identify parallelism and understand its uses.

2. Adding Parallelism. Take a loose-jointed student or professional essay and ask students to make the sentences denser by adding parallelism wherever possible. Ask them to decide when the parallelism adds to the essay and when it detracts.

3. Patterns for Parallelism. Ask students to write sentences containing correlative conjunctions, lists, and coordinate structures that require parallelism. Tell students to vary the sentences as much as they can in content and in use of parallelism.

Chapter 18 "Emphasizing Main Ideas"

Chapter 18 concentrates on achieving emphasis within sentences by the distribution of information and the choice of strategies to achieve a particular effect. A special feature of the chapter is its treatment of cumulative and periodic sentences, a discussion that stresses the rhetorical impact of each sentence pattern. The sentence-combining exercises that accompany the discussion are designed to help students feel comfortable using these patterns in their

writing. The opening discussion also looks at the importance
of sentence beginnings and endings and at the effective
arrangement of items in a series. Most students benefit from
some work with these basic ways of controlling emphasis as
well as from discussion of using the active voice (18d) and
of being concise (18e). Students who have problems with sentence structure, however, may have more difficulty with the
effective uses of repetition (18b) and separation (18c) for
emphasis.

Activities and Assignments

1. <u>More Combining</u>. Give students a list of information
about a topic and ask them to combine it to emphasize certain
features or to achieve a particular rhetorical purpose.

2. <u>Rewrite</u>. Take a passage from a student or professional essay and ask students to rewrite it, using different sentence patterns that give different emphasis to the
content of the sentences. Split the students into groups and
have them compare their versions with the original, trying to
identify a new version that is in some ways clearer than the
original and that contains more appropriate emphasis on the
main ideas. Since students may well have decided to emphasize different ideas than did the original passage, the discussion may get into matters of content as well as style.

3. <u>Clear Up the Confusion</u>. Choose a particularly
confusing or unemphatic passage from a student essay, give it
to the class, and ask what devices covered in the chapter
could be used to improve the passage. Decide on changes as a
group and write the revised passage on the board.

Chapter 19 "Achieving Variety"

The chapter on sentence variety is partly a summary of
the preceding three chapters in that it asks students to
think of sentences not as single units but as a sequence of
ideas working together. Coordination, subordination,
parallelism, and emphasis all come into play in the examples
in the chapter. You will probably want to emphasize the
introduction to this chapter and sections 19a (on varying
length and structure of sentences) and 19b (on varying
sentence beginnings). At the same time, you may wish to pay
somewhat less attention to sections 19c and 19d, which
briefly describe the occasional uses of inverted sentence
order and of minor sentence types such as questions and
commands.

Activities and Assignments

The activities for the preceding chapter can be easily adapted for this chapter. You may also wish to try the following activities:

1. Simple Sentences. Take a professional or student essay, reduce it to simple sentences, and ask students to rewrite it, adding variety. Then ask them to compare their versions to the original.

2. Using Forms. Tell students to write a paragraph making use of the strategies suggested in this chapter. Leave the content of the paragraph up to them; they will discover how form can help suggest content.

PART V PUNCTUATION

Chapters 20 to 25   "End Punctuation"; "The Comma"; "The Semicolon"; "The Apostrophe"; "Quotation Marks"; "Other Punctuation Marks"

This part of the Handbook has been organized for convenient reference: The first chapter (20) brings together the uses of the three marks of end punctuation; the next four chapters address the uses of the comma (21), the semicolon (22), the apostrophe (23), and quotation marks (24); and the final chapter (25) deals with the less-used marks (colon, dashes, parentheses, brackets, ellipsis mark, slash). Each principal use of each mark is assigned a separate heading and section.

The use you make of these chapters will depend partly on your students and partly on whether you choose to use the chapters solely to teach punctuation or as part of a sentence-combining program. Well-prepared college students should need no formal instruction in punctuation, although they, like all of us, will need to check on particular conventions as they write. Other students may require specific work with the principal uses of the comma, the semicolon, and the apostrophe, and some students may profit from a review of end punctuation. Almost all students, however, find punctuation of restrictive and nonrestrictive elements a problem, and the extensive discussion in 21c should prove helpful. Two special features of this discussion are the practical tests for determining if an element is restrictive or nonrestrictive and the discussion of how the context of a sentence helps determine the role an element plays.

The sentence-combining exercises in Chapters 21 and 22 give students a chance to practice using the comma and the semicolon. They also ask students to create sentences with the structures these marks of punctuation make possible, such as independent clauses joined with a semicolon, nonrestrictive clauses and phrases, introductory clauses and phrases, and compound sentences. By asking students to complete these exercises, an instructor can encourage variety in sentence structure and style.

If time allows, you may wish to point out to your class how punctuation marks often substitute for other grammatical and semantic signals used in speech. Students may also see that punctuation is not invented to confuse and burden them if they understand that it has four principal functions: (1) marking the ends of main clauses, including those standing alone as sentences and those joined in compound sentences; (2) distinguishing subordinate elements (primarily introductory, nonrestrictive, and parenthetical elements) from the main sentence pattern; (3) separating coordinate elements; and (4) setting off or separating dates, times, quotations, and the like.

Activities and Assignments

1. _Sample Papers._ Revise all or part of one of the sample papers presented in Chapter 3 of this _Manual_ ("Evaluating Student Essays") to introduce punctuation errors of the kind you have been emphasizing in class. Distribute copies of the altered paper and ask students to correct it. You may also wish to use a student paper.

2. _Group Proofreading._ On the day papers are due, ask students to form small groups and to proofread one another's papers, identifying errors by circling them, but not correcting them. Ask the authors to correct their own errors and to turn to the group or the teacher for general advice. This activity should not be repeated too often lest students come to rely on the group to find their errors.

3. _Restrictive and Nonrestrictive Pairs._ Give students a sentence containing a modifying element and ask them to write two brief groups of sentences, one providing a context that requires that the element in the original sentence be restrictive, another requiring a nonrestrictive element.

4. _Creating Sentences._ Choose a mark of punctuation you wish to emphasize in class, the semicolon perhaps, and

ask students to write sentences using the punctuation correctly. You may wish to use this activity as a quiz.

5. Repunctuating. Take an essay from a reader or a similar source, remove the punctuation you wish to emphasize, make copies of the essay, and ask students to punctuate it. When students have finished, they can compare their work to the original.

PART VI MECHANICS

Chapters 26 to 30 "Capitals"; "Italics"; "Abbreviations"; "Numbers"; "Word Division"

Some of the observations made about punctuation obviously apply to mechanics, whose conventions have no equivalent in speech. These chapters, like those on punctuation, are organized for convenient reference. You may wish to emphasize that although matters of mechanics are entirely conventional, observing the conventions is, nonetheless, a part of any writer's responsibility to readers. Attention to minor detail is an important part of any task.

Activities and Assignments

1. Add the Mechanics. Take an essay, either student or professional; remove capitals, italics, and the like; and ask students to correct the mechanics in the "new" essay. When the students are finished, they can compare their work to the original.

2. Quizzes. Have students look through the chapters in this section and write questions for a quiz on mechanics. Divide the students into groups and have each group choose the toughest questions its members have written and assemble a quiz. Ask groups to exchange quizzes and take the tests. At the end you may want to indicate which group wrote the toughest quiz and which did the best job answering questions.

PART VII EFFECTIVE WORDS

Perhaps more than with any other section of the Handbook, the use you make of Part VII will depend on your interests. If you want students to examine language for its own sake, you may wish to expand on the material in the first section of Chapter 31 to stress the roles played by geographical, social, and occupational dialects and to emphasize the integrity of every dialect for its own speakers. Or you may wish to emphasize the basic symbolic nature of all language, expanding the discussions in 31b of denotation and connotation and of abstract and concrete, general and specific language. Chapter 32, on the dictionary, could become the basis of an entire course unit on that important source of information. The necessarily brief treatment of the historical development of the English language, incorporated in Chapter 33 on vocabulary development, could be supplemented with a discussion of how language constantly changes. And Chapter 34 on spelling could be used for individual or in-class reviews and drill.

Chapter 31 "Controlling Diction"

Chapter 31 is, of course, the basic chapter of Part VII. The chapter deals successively with appropriate usage (31a), exactness (31b), and conciseness (31c). Of course, no instructional shortcut can substitute for experience in choosing the appropriate word, in knowing when slang or a colloquialism is actually more effective than a standard word or expression, or in deciding when a technical term is useful or requires definition. But students are often interested in such matters, and some class time may usefully be spent considering how alternative choices affect their own sentences or paragraphs as well as sample sentences such as those in Exercise 1 (p. 387). Similarly, the topics in 31b--abstract and concrete words, general and specific words, and the connotations of words--often generate lively class discussion. Although it is no substitute for the reading and practice that cultivate a reliable feeling for words and their shades of meaning, such discussion can sometimes stimulate an interest in words that leads to close attention to them.

Conciseness, addressed in section 31c, frequently causes problems for students, who are likely to mistake brevity for conciseness and to confuse simple lack of development with economy. Some practice with the ways to simplify sentences and word groups, such as those discussed in section 31c-3, can be useful, as can attention to the empty words and phrases and to the unnecessary repetition that are more obvious sources of flabbiness in writing.

Activities and Assignments

1. Cutting Words. Before your students hand in their essays, ask them to cut a specific number of words (ten to fifteen for a start) without harming the meaning. This can work with paragraphs as well and makes a good small-group activity.

2. Fill in the Blanks. Distribute an essay with important words deleted, and ask students to fill in the blanks with the best words they can find. Discuss the choices in class as a way of building students' vocabularies and of deciding questions of appropriateness and exactness.

3. Personal Responses. Give students a list of words and ask them to write out the personal connotations of each word. Asking them to share their responses with the class may further help them understand the potential richness of language.

4. Rewrite. Give students a particularly wordy sentence and ask them to see who can rewrite it using the fewest words. This activity also works with whole paragraphs and can be used in small groups.

Chapter 32 "Using the Dictionary"

Chapter 32 describes the information provided in a good dictionary, summarizes briefly the characteristics of several widely used desk dictionaries and some unabridged and special dictionaries, and explains typical entries from two abridged dictionaries to help students find information. Although the unavoidable accumulation of detail in such a brief chapter makes dense reading in places, the chapter is organized for easy reference so that you and your students can single out the most useful sections. Throughout the Handbook, students are urged to consult a dictionary for answers to particular questions—the right preposition to use in an idiom, the usage status of a word, the forms of an irregular verb, and the like. No other supplementary reference will serve students as well as a good desk dictionary, as long as they know how to use it and do so. Whenever practicable, they should be required to purchase one of the standard desk dictionaries.

A Guide to The Little, Brown Handbook

Chapters 33 and 34 "Improving Your Vocabulary"; "Spelling"

The chapters on vocabulary and spelling will benefit some students a great deal and others perhaps not at all. Most students can profit from systematic attention to improving their vocabulary, but the course time available for such attention is often very limited. Special workbooks are available, of course, for students with basic vocabulary problems. Chapter 33 provides a good introduction to vocabulary building for students who wish to enrich their vocabularies and suggests activities you may wish to assign. After glancing at the development of the English language and the variety of sources from which our rich vocabulary is drawn (33a), the chapter looks at the roots, prefixes, and suffixes of words (33b), at ways to learn new words from their context, and at the value of habitually consulting a dictionary--the best methods of gradually and continually expanding vocabulary while reading.

No quick formula exists for turning poor spellers into good spellers. Students with very serious spelling problems may need systematic instruction, which, like systematic vocabulary instruction, course time rarely allows. You may want to refer such students to a skills center on campus or, if there are no such facilities, to a good spelling workbook. There are, however, activities and assignments that can help. Most students can improve their spelling markedly by learning and actually applying the limited number of standard rules, by maintaining a record of words that repeatedly cause them trouble, and by faithfully practicing brief groups of words from a spelling list. Such advice, though uninspired and unoriginal, does produce real improvement if a student can be persuaded to follow it, perhaps with the added reminder that lack of confidence in spelling distracts the student from more important matters in writing.

PART VIII SPECIAL WRITING ASSIGNMENTS

Chapter 35 "Writing a Research Paper"

Chapter 35 traces the process of preparing an investigative paper, from the initial decision on a manageable topic to the actual writing, revising, and documenting of the paper. The chapter concludes with a representative student paper, "How Advertisers Make Us Buy," which is annotated with comments on the facing pages. The models for bibliographical entries (pp. 461-65) and footnote entries (pp. 481-86), as well as the recommendations for manuscript form, are based on the MLA Handbook (1977), a sound and usable source and also the one most likely to be familiar to composition instructors. The chapter also includes models based on the widely used <u>Publications Manual of the American Psychological Association</u> (pp. 465-66 and 487-89) as well as the form of citation used in the sciences. Students should be alerted to the varying styles of documentation, and they may need help in understanding that the community they eventually work in and write for will require its own standard style.

The research paper can easily become—and perhaps too often is—little more than a burdensome, time-consuming task for a student, an extended exercise in observing the conventions of documentation. But it can also be a constructive and rewarding project, so long as students have enough time to do the preliminary reading necessary for a clear topic to evolve; to accumulate information from at least a few different sources; and to draft, carefully revise, and document the paper. Your students' success may depend on your having adequate time and energy to guide them through what is, even for a paper of a few pages, a very complicated task.

With reasonable time and guidance, students can gain from writing a research paper not only a sense of accomplishment but also an experience that can serve them well in later writing assignments. In contrast to a short essay, the longer research paper requires more complex development and organization. Thus a carefully planned outline and a body of accessible notes become more self-evidently useful. The way a clearly defined topic and thesis statement almost necessarily evolve through reading, prewriting, writing, and revising becomes more apparent and understandable. The fact that some topics work and others just don't, that some questions and issues are usefully discussable and others are not, is itself a valuable intellectual discovery more likely to be made during writing a research paper than during any other kind of writing. Of course, research itself gives students a firmer grasp of the range of information and carefully reasoned judgments, many of them conflicting, that exist on most issues. And preparing a research paper gives students a valuable lesson in the need for intellectual honesty and meticulous attention to detail in recording sources.

These are admittedly ambitious and doubtless idealized goals. If you have taught the research paper before, you know that the extent to which such goals are realized depends greatly on the help students receive at the major steps along the way. Most students need particular help in selecting a researchable topic, in locating the most useful references from which to work, in note taking, and in understanding the purposes of documentation. You may wish to assign Exercises

1, 2, 5, 6, 9, 11, 12, 14, and 15, which ask students to perform a definite task at each step in the development of their own topic and can serve as a series of checkpoints for you. The sample student paper at the end of the chapter, with its accompanying comments, can be used as a basis for class discussion before students turn to writing and revising their own papers. The sample paper is essentially sound, more than merely competent as a student paper but by no means above criticism.

Chapter 36 "Practical Writing"

The two brief sections of Chapter 36 offer simple, commonsense advice about writing essay answers for examinations and basic guidance in the form and content of business letters and memos, including the letter of application. You may let this chapter stand as a useful reference for students; or you may choose to devote course time to one or both of its topics. Some students respond well to specific assignments in these areas because their usefulness to their immediate future is self-evident.

APPENDIXES AND GLOSSARIES

Appendixes A, B, and C "Avoiding Plagiarism"; "Preparing a Manuscript"; "Improving Study Skills"

A discussion of plagiarism (Appendix A) and the specifications for the form of a manuscript (Appendix B) seem useful for all writing that students do. Hence these sections are placed as appendixes, where they are easily accessible and where they do not interfere with the flow of other, dissimilar kinds of information earlier in the text. The material on plagiarism defines, advises, and warns. The appendix does not deal explicitly with the highly varied and self-evident problems of deliberate plagiarism from sources or from other students' work. Instead, it attempts to prevent inadvertent plagiarism that is born of naiveté. It provides guidance on what kinds of information must be acknowledged and on quoting, paraphrasing, or summarizing both consciously (with acknowledgment) and fairly. You will want to underscore or add to these basic guidelines according to your own students and expectations.

The information on manuscript preparation is standard and will cover most manuscript situations. It deals only with the physical form of the handwritten or typewritten manuscript. Such matters as revision of manuscript drafts, instructors' correction systems, and word division are treated where they are more directly relevant (Chapter 2 for the first two; Chapter 30 for the third). Appendix B leaves open the possibility of other formats, so you may wish to modify its details according to your preferences or the requirements of the course.

The final appendix (C), on improving study skills, is intended to help students who are not well prepared for college, having no clear conception of serious study and no habits of regular and orderly procedure. The appendix consists merely of common sense and common knowledge. Nonetheless, students who are willing should benefit from the practical advice on reading effectively, taking good notes in class, studying for examinations, and the like.

"Glossary of Usage"; "Glossary of Grammatical Terms"

The glossaries of usage and of terms are mostly self-explanatory. The Glossary of Usage is at the back of the book rather than among other sections dealing with the use of words, for easier reference. Space prohibits incorporating anything like a complete usage glossary in a handbook. The more than 200 words and word pairs provided in this glossary are those that cause students the most problems. Inevitably, however, many students will need to consult a good desk dictionary to resolve usage questions.

The Handbook consistently provides clear definitions, with examples, of all grammatical terms when they are introduced (in boldface type) and then redefines them or refers to the original definition whenever they come up again. These in-text definitions mean that students who dip into the Handbook do not have to search unnecessarily for the meanings of the words they encounter. But when students want only the meaning of a term or an illustration of it, the Glossary of Terms is a handy reference. To broaden its use as a course reference, the glossary includes definitions not only of all terms used in the text but also of some terms that students may meet elsewhere or that you may introduce.

CHAPTER 3

EVALUATING STUDENT ESSAYS

Nothing we do as composition teachers--not lecturing, leading discussions, or arranging classroom activities--has the same potential for helping students improve their writing as do our responses as sensitive and thorough readers. Our responses can help students judge the success of particular writing strategies, recognize problems in grammar and punctuation, and discover how another person reacts to their ideas. Yet evaluating student papers can be a time-consuming job: Instructors often report spending fifteen to twenty minutes on each paper making marginal notes, writing summary comments, and deciding on a grade. To help make the job of grading papers a bit easier and quicker, The Little, Brown Handbook provides a number of aids: a number-and-letter correction code that refers students to appropriate sections of the Handbook, a list of correction symbols keyed to discussions in the text, and a thorough index and glossary of grammatical terms directing students to explanations of terms used in an instructor's written comments.

It takes more than an efficient correction system to bring about improvement in writing, however. So that students do not continually introduce the same errors into their papers or have the same problems with development and organization, we need to make sure that they understand the symbols or vocabulary we use in commenting on their essays. We also need to give our comments a positive, helpful tone and a clear focus so that students can apply what we have to say to their writing. Finally, we need to make sure that the grades we assign accurately reflect the quality of the papers and give students a distinct idea of the goals for their writing. In all these areas, too, The Little, Brown Handbook can be a valuable resource.

THREE APPROACHES TO COMMENTING ON PAPERS

Though composition instructors have developed a number of innovative and useful ways of evaluating student writing, including conferences, tape-recorded commentary, and peer evaluations, most teachers still prefer to respond to student essays through marginal and summary comments. These responses take three general forms: a number-and-letter correction code, correction symbols, and written comments. Each method has advantages and disadvantages.

To use the correction code, an instructor simply writes in the margin of a paper the number and letter of the section of The Little, Brown Handbook the student should consult for help with a particular problem or error--for example, 8b (pronoun and antecedent agreement), 11a (comma splice), or 1d (problem with thesis). The code for each section of the Handbook is listed inside the back cover; after a short time, most instructors find they have memorized the codes for common problems and only occasionally have to consult the list.

Chapter 2 of the Handbook contains a sample student paper (Linda Balik's comparison essay) graded using the correction code; here is part of another paper:

> Parents have become more lenient with regard to
> television watching. *For example, allowing their* (10)
> (B3) children to watch cartoon in the (early morning (31c)
> before school). As soon as they come home from
> (21b) school they sit before the set again, completely (31b)
> (34a) (ingrossed) (with) a soap opera or a talk show. Some
> parents actually allow their children to watch
> television while (they) are at the supper table. (12a)
> Of course, the latter part of the evening, the
> prime time, is (solely) set aside for the purpose (14c)
> of watching a special show or a favorite series.
> In some ways, parents are using the television as
> a substitute for personal communication with the
> (2/c) child. The days then, remain a never ending (34d)
> chain of program after program.

When students get their graded papers back, they need only to turn to the back of the Handbook to understand what the instructor's notations mean and to the appropriate section of the text for a full explanation (the code for each section appears in colored boxes on the sides of the pages).

Students, too, quickly learn to recognize the notations for common errors and problems.

Correction symbols work in much the same way as the number-and-letter code. An instructor locates the appropriate symbol in the list inside the front cover of the Handbook (dev, log, agr, coh, and so on) and writes it in the margin of the essay, often drawing a line to indicate the location and extent of the problem. Students reverse the process, looking up symbols on the list, which also contains the name of the problem and a reference to the appropriate section of the text: for example, dm--Dangling modifier, 14g. Chapter 2 of the Handbook contains a paragraph from student Linda Balik's essay marked with symbols. Here, in addition, is the passage from above marked in this way.

Parents have become more lenient with regard to television watching. For example, allowing their children to watch cartoon in the early morning *frag* before school. As soon as they come home from *rep* school they sit before the set again, completely *P* ingrossed with a soap opera or a talk show. Some *sp* parents actually allow their children to watch television while they are at the supper table. *ref* Of course, the latter part of the evening, the *mm* prime time, is solely set aside for the purpose of watching a special show or a favorite series. In some ways, parents are using the television as a substitute for personal communication with the *P* child. The days then, remain a neveroending *hyph* chain of program after program.

Correction symbols are easier to remember than the number-and-letter code, so both students and teachers can spend less time turning away from a paper to consult the list of symbols than they might do with the code. Yet symbols are less specific than the code; shift, for instance, covers a variety of problems--13a (person and number), 13b (tense and mood), 13c (subject and voice), and 13d (indirect and direct discourse). Moreover, instead of being able to turn directly from the paper to a discussion in the Handbook, students may need to consult the list of symbols to find the appropriate section of the text. The symbols, however, also appear in the colored boxes in the margins of the pages.

Although using a correction code or correction symbols can be an efficient way to grade papers, some instructors prefer comments with a more personal touch than letters and numbers or symbols. In addition, while the need to have the Handbook at hand to understand the instructor's comments may be an advantage for most students, some--perhaps those who need help the most--may put off reviewing their papers or ignore the job entirely because of the effort involved. If you choose to use the code or symbols, you should remember also that there is nothing in either system to let students know they have done a good job on a particular passage and nothing to encourage them to do a thorough job of looking up explanations in the Handbook. To praise good work and make sure students turn to the Handbook for help, you will have to rely on written or oral comments. You may also wish to require students to do exercises in the text and hand them in.

Written comments take a good deal more time than symbols or the correction code. Yet written comments allow the instructor to address the specific problems in an essay, not just to indicate a general type of problem. For example, even though the symbol mng ("meaning unclear") may be an accurate response, the following written comment tells the student writer much more about the need to communicate clearly with an audience: "I've read this several times and I still can't figure out which side you agree with on this issue--or if you are just trying to avoid taking a stand." Moreover, written comments give the teacher a chance to praise successful passages.

Written comments can be specific and helpful, but they are not likely to be as detailed as explanations in the Handbook. Some instructors, therefore, combine grading systems by making references to relevant sections of the Handbook part of their written comments on serious problems--"This passage is hard to follow because of the loose way you use that and which. See 12c." Without such a reference, the student who wants more help than the comment gives may have to rely on the glossary of grammatical terms, the index, or the table of contents to locate an appropriate explanation. This procedure will work only if the student already knows something about the problem or if the instructor has used a term that also appears in the glossary or index. By combining the correction code with written comments, however, an instructor can provide the necessary guidance.

Another reason for combining methods of grading is that a system may be better suited to some kinds of problems than to others. For example, most instructors would prefer to

write 21a in the margin rather than "You need a comma before
and connecting main clauses"--particularly if the error
occurs again and again in an essay. And // is more direct
and can be just as effective as the comment "You need to make
the elements in this sentence parallel." Yet when brevity is
less important, when a symbol doesn't say enough, or when the
problem is peculiar to an essay and no reference to the
Handbook is possible or desirable, a written comment is
appropriate.

Here is a selection from a student paper graded using
written comments combined with symbols and the correction
code:

> One cause of student stress and probably the
> most common is academic (pressures). College
> academics create so much stress on a student
> that every college campus in America should be
> required to have free psychiatric counseling
> available. The pressure on a student from his
> or her workload is incredible. The pressure
> just doesn't occur during mid-terms and finals
> but occurs all semester, also. The constant
> pressure to do well and to keep from falling
> behind is always present.
>
> Parent and peer pressure also increases the
> amount of stress a student must indure, parents
> and friends are always reminding of the
> importance of academic success. Parents bring
> up the importance of academic success not only
> for reasons of acheivement but also reminding
> the student of who is paying the tuition.

Handwritten margin notes: pressure? this sounds like a conclusion. It might work better below. You might decide to combine the paragraphs, too. — ww — psychological? — w — sp — the student — no comma — good point — 11a — 17a

No matter what single method of commenting you choose,
or whether, like many instructors, you decide to combine the
methods, it is usually important to provide students with a
summary comment at the end of their papers to give an explanation of the grade and to tie together the marginal commentary, emphasizing the most important points. This is also
a good place to assign exercises in the Handbook and to remind students what they need to do in future essays. The

discussion later in this chapter, "Evaluating Essays for a Grade," contains several examples of summary comments.

MAKING SURE STUDENTS UNDERSTAND YOUR COMMENTS

Having chosen a method for commenting on papers, you need to make sure that your students understand your system; unless they do, the time you spend grading papers will be largely wasted. Perhaps the most common reason students fail to understand our comments is that they do not understand the symbols or terms we use. Many students, for example, know what a sentence fragment is, but if you were to ask a class what a run-on sentence is, most of the students would probably answer in this vein: "a sentence that is too long—one that goes on and on." Terms like "reference," "development," and "parallelism" would also be likely to draw puzzled or incorrect responses, although a few students might be able to give general explanations of the terms. Asking students the meaning of common symbols like <u>pass</u>, <u>cs</u>, <u>dm</u>, and <u>//</u> would produce similar results.

Telling students to look up correction marks on the front or back endpapers of the <u>Handbook</u> can help, as can alerting them to the glossary of grammatical terms or handing out a list of terms you plan to use in written comments. A lot of students, however, are likely to put off learning the symbols or terms until they absolutely have to, several papers into the semester when they realize how much help they need to improve their writing.

A more effective way to alert students to the need to understand your correction system and at the same time to find out how much they already know is to quiz them on the terms or symbols you will be using. Here are some sample questions:

> What is parallelism? Give an example.
> Define "run-on sentence," and give an example.
> What does each of these symbols mean: <u>frag</u>,
> <u>dm</u>, <u>ww</u>, <u>t</u>, <u>agr</u>, <u>//</u>, and <u>ref</u>?

The misconceptions that surface on a quiz can be an aid to instruction. For example, students who think run-ons are overlong sentences are likely to respond to criticism of run-ons in their work by writing short, choppy sentences. The teacher who has spotted the potential misunderstanding can point out in class discussion that run-ons are caused by a failure to recognize sentence boundaries and to punctuate them correctly, not by the length of sentences. Comments on papers can also be expanded in an appropriate manner: "There are a lot of run-ons in this paper. Make sure you know what a run-on is by reading section 11c in the Handbook and by doing Exercises 2 and 3."

Another good way to help students understand your comments is to discuss a marked paper with them. Chapter 2 of the Handbook contains an example of a marked paper that you may wish to use as the basis of class discussion. In addition, the following paragraphs contain many errors of the kind likely to turn up on student papers. The paragraphs can be distributed in class either with the marking symbols used below or some other system you prefer. If you choose to distribute the paragraphs without markings, you can ask the students to work with you in identifying errors and choosing appropriate symbols or comments.

(20c) When you were little did you ever stare at a disabled child. Many children do and are often ? p.
punished because of it. Staring is just a form
(34a) of curiousity, the child wants to learn more or sp
observe the handicapped child's ways. Mainstreaming handicapped children into a regular
(31b) classroom can fulfill the curiosity of the nor- ww
mal child. Before a handicapped child is inter- sp
(34a) grated into a classroom, the teacher should provide the students in the class with information
(31c) about the handicapped child. This will bring a w
little ease when the child is first brought into ww
(31b) the class. A complete lesson on disabilities
(18d) should be taught, thus providing students with pass
learning experiences that will dampen ignorance.
Teachers may also point out differences in all
children, even the differences between normal gr/ww
(21b) children. Through mainstreaming, children will p
(83) also become interested in how or why a disabled
child does what he does. Once the handicapped
child is accepted, the normal children will ask
questions, thus enhancing the understanding of p
individual differences in all people.

(34a) Before the _intergration_ of handicapped chil- *sp*
dren with normal children came about in 1977,
(12) many children did not socially accept a handi- *ref*
(11a) capped child. They taunted them, some still do. *cs*
In some states, including New Jersey, Illinois,
and Texas, handicapped children have been going
to school with normal children for years. Many
schools offer programs where the handicapped
(14c) students go _only_ to school part time. They *mm*
attend classes that are suited for thilr needs. *typo?*
(27a) In 1976, Time carried a story about Danny *ital*
Kodmur, 11, a child with cerebral palsy. He
attended a special school until he was ten years
(22e) of age; and began to attend Cheremoya Elementary *no;*
School in Los Angeles at 11. In his first year
of school, he was elected president of his
(31c-2) student body by the student body. *rep*

FOCUSED, POSITIVE COMMENTARY

Noting errors is one part of grading; the other parts,
just as important, are praising successes and suggesting ways
to improve future work. Positive commentary, even outright
praise, identifies for students those writing strategies that
succeeded and at the same time motivates them to try just as
hard, or perhaps harder, on the next writing assignment. In
addition, it helps student writers develop a sense of audience, so that they see readers as people who can be reached
and pleased by good writing, not simply as fault-finders.
Praise need not be excessive to be effective. A "good" written in the margin next to a successful sentence or paragraph
or a personal response--"I like the topic of this essay"--
written in a summary comment can do a great deal. Comments
that take into account both the strengths and the weaknesses
in a paper can be particularly effective because they suggest
ways the writer can revise the paper or do better on the next
assignment: "The preceding paragraphs were not well developed, but this one contains a good example and a lot of in-

teresting detail. The paragraph grabs the reader's attention and holds it."

To be useful to student writers, comments need to be clearly focused. In class, we encourage students to limit their topics, to make sure their writing has a clear point, or thesis, and to distinguish more important ideas from less important ones. When it comes to grading papers, though, instructors can forget to apply these principles to their own work. The results are diffuse summary comments that fail to highlight the important strengths and weaknesses in a paper, or marginal comments that treat all the errors in a paper as if they were roughly equal, leading students to misunderstand the contribution of each to the final grade. Unfocused comments are often the result of praiseworthy intentions: The teacher wants to make sure the student is aware of all the areas that need improvement in his or her writing and, in addition, wants to maintain high standards for expression. The student, however, does not benefit from the commentary because it gives no clear direction for future writing efforts.

Two ways to avoid the problem of unfocused commentary are to make selective comments and to make comments that establish priorities for future writing. Selective commentary assumes that errors vary in importance depending on the particular assignment, the goals of the course, or the student's progress. Selective commentary on a narrative or descriptive paper, for example, might focus on the presence or absence of vivid, concrete detail. In grading an argumentative essay, however, an instructor might pay primary attention to thesis, adequate support, and transitions. If class discussion has placed considerable emphasis on avoiding fragments and run-ons and has paid relatively little attention to reference problems, the instructor's commentary might take note only of the most serious reference problems, those that are particularly confusing or irritating. Of course, after the class has discussed pronoun reference, the instructor would begin attending to it when marking papers.

Other assumptions behind selective commentary are that it is difficult for students (and the rest of us) to pay attention to more than one major job at a time and that students who are having the most trouble with their writing may also have trouble understanding elements that have not been reviewed in class. Thus, while A or B students with only a few minor marks on their papers--ref, sp, ww--can be expected to profit from looking up all the problem areas on their own in the Handbook, weaker students with ten or fifteen serious errors marked in their essays--frag, agr, log, shift, coh, dev--need the combined assistance of lecture, discussion, and readings and exercises in the Handbook. They will also need time to come to grips with the many different problems in their writing.

In addition, students who see a host of grammar, punctuation, and usage errors marked on a paper may assume that these are the most important problems in their writing and may pay less attention to matters such as thesis, development, and organization. Or, having corrected sentence-level problems, they may be unwilling to undertake large-scale revision that would require throwing out the very sentences they have just worked so hard to fix.

Yet one might argue that students have to learn to pay attention to all the problems in their writing and that to ignore some errors in a student's paper, whatever the reason, may be to send a misleading signal. Even instructors who find selective commentary useful may find it difficult to refrain from making extensive notations on some papers, feeling that it is their responsibility to alert the students to serious communication problems. For these instructors, the solution may be to establish priorities for the way students are to understand and respond to the instructor's comments. A system of priorities allows the instructor to point out all the problem areas in a paper while at the same time directing students' attention to the most important kinds of problems.

Perhaps the easiest way to establish priorities is to use the summary comment to identify the most serious problems (and strengths, too) and then to suggest concrete steps for solving the problems through revision or in future papers. Here are two examples of such comments:

> . . . The most serious problem in this essay is the lack of development in the paragraphs. You need many more extended examples to support your point about the role of computers in all levels of education. But the many comma splices in the paper are also an important problem because they are so distracting to a reader. I have taken note of comma splices in determining the grade; work on avoiding them in your next paper because they will count even more heavily in the grade. The other problems noted in the margins—14g, etc.—occur less consistently and do not interfere as much with the

reader's perception of your meaning and enjoyment
of your essay. Look them up in the <u>Handbook</u>,
however, and watch for them as you proofread your
next essay.

. . . .

Your topic and your point of view on it are
very intriguing. But the lack of concrete detail
at the places I have noted weakens the essay.
Work to add detail as you revise. The problems
in logic in the fourth paragraph are important
and need to be dealt with if you decide to retain
the preceding paragraph (see 4d-3 in the <u>Hand-
book</u>). After you have completed these more
substantial revisions, look for problems in
pronoun reference, which make many of your
sentences confusing. (Do Exercises 1 and 2 in
Chapter 12 of the <u>Handbook</u>.) Check on the other
problems noted in the body of the paper, and be
sure to correct the spelling errors before you
hand in the revised essay for a final grade.

Many instructors read student essays twice, the first
time to identify general strengths and weaknesses, the second
time to write comments praising successful passages and indicating areas that need more work. Other instructors decide
ahead of time what elements of the assignment or course are
most important and try to restrict their comments to these.
But while the latter procedure saves a bit of time, it will
not be successful unless both the teacher and the students
understand the aims for the assignment and the grading standards in the course. Making the goals of the course clear is
a good procedure because it provides a firm basis for
evaluation.

EVALUATING ESSAYS FOR A GRADE

A grade can carry several messages: It can describe the overall quality of a paper; it can indicate how close the essay comes to achieving the goals for writing set forth in the course; and it can help tell a student writer what elements to work on in the next assignment. But unless grading standards are clear, the grades we assign will have little value for teaching beyond establishing a final grade for the course.

To help establish clear evaluation standards, many instructors discuss grading criteria with students and distribute sample papers, either already graded or to be graded in class. Another method is to attach to each paper a comment sheet that reflects the goals for the assignment. Preparing a comment sheet for each assignment can be taxing, however, so many instructors prepare a sheet that can be used for all assignments. Here are two samples, each of which uses a different set of grading criteria:

Thesis:

Organization:

Development:

Grammar and
  Punctuation:

Style:

Comment/Grade:

These are the areas where
your paper is

strong   weak

	thesis	
	development	
	paragraphs	
	sentences	
	grammar	
	word choice	
	punctuation	
	style	

Comment/Grade:

If you do not like to use comment sheets, you may prefer
to hand out grading criteria at the beginning of the course.
Sometimes a department or program provides its own set of
criteria for grading papers; if yours does not, you may wish
to adapt for your own use the following set that reflects the
major areas of emphasis in The Little, Brown Handbook:

A (Superior)—An A paper meets the standards in all these
    areas and excels in one or more areas:
        The paper as a whole presents a fresh subject or
        central idea or treats it in an interesting or orig-

69

inal manner, displaying unusual insight. The paper
has a clear pattern appropriate to its purpose and
uses a variety of rhetorical strategies. The tone
is appropriate to the audience. The paragraphs are
fully developed with detail that supports the central idea; sentences within the paragraphs are
clearly linked, forming an appropriate pattern;
transitions are effective. Sentences are varied and
imaginative in style, concise and creative in wording. The paper contains few errors in grammar and
punctuation or errors only in sophisticated matters,
and few spelling errors.

B (Strong)—A B paper meets the standards in all these
areas:

The paper as a whole presents an interesting subject
or central idea and approaches it in a consistent
and careful manner, displaying good insight, though
without the freshness or originality characteristic
of the A paper. The pattern of the essay is appropriate to its purpose and the writing makes use of
consistent rhetorical strategies and a tone appropriate to the audience. Paragraphs are, with only a
few exceptions, adequately developed and generally
successful in supporting the central idea; transitions are clear, and sentences within the paragraphs
are, for the most part, clearly related. Sentences
are clear and correct in structure and style and are
not excessively wordy. Word choice is usually
appropriate. Grammar, punctuation, and spelling
follow accepted conventions except for a few minor
errors.

C (Adequate)—A C paper is seriously deficient in one of
these areas:

The paper as a whole presents a clearly defined
subject or central idea, but the treatment may be
trivial, uninteresting, or too general, and the
insight adequate but not marked by independent
thought. The plan and purpose are clear but inconsistently or incompletely carried out; tone may be
inconsistent. Some paragraphs may lack adequate
supporting detail or may be only loosely linked to
the central idea. Sentences within paragraphs may
be only loosely related, and some transitions may be
missing. Sentences are generally correct in
structure but may be excessively wordy, vague, or,
at times, even incorrect. Style and word choice may
be flat, inconsistent, or not entirely appropriate
to the audience. The paper may contain isolated
serious errors in grammar and punctuation or fre-

quent minor errors that do not interfere substantially with meaning or that do not greatly distract the reader; the paper may contain occasional <u>misspellings.</u>

<u>D</u> (Weak)--A <u>D</u> paper is seriously deficient in any one of these areas:

The <u>paper as a whole</u> presents a poorly defined or inconsistently treated subject or central idea and displays little insight. The plan and purpose are not treated consistently. The tone is inappropriate to the audience. <u>Paragraphs</u> contain little supporting detail or inappropriate detail and are often unrelated to the central idea. Sentences within paragraphs are often unrelated and transitions are lacking. <u>Sentences</u> are frequently incorrect in structure, vague, wordy, and distracting. Style and word choice are inappropriate, incorrect, or inconsistent. The paper may contain serious and distracting errors in <u>grammar and punctuation</u> as well as numerous irritating minor errors and frequent <u>misspellings.</u>

<u>F</u> (Unacceptable/No Credit)--An <u>F</u> paper is unacceptable in any one of these areas:

The <u>paper as a whole</u> does not have a clear subject or central idea and has no apparent purpose or plan; <u>or</u> the subject and central idea are defined and treated in a way that clearly does not meet the requirements of the assignment. <u>Paragraphs</u> are not related to the central idea; sentences within paragraphs are unrelated, and transitions are missing. <u>Sentences</u> are so faulty in structure and style that the essay is not readable. Frequent serious errors in <u>grammar, punctuation, and spelling</u> indicate an inability to handle the written conventions; there are excessive minor errors or misspellings.

These criteria need to be adapted to the level of students in a particular course or institution and to the goals set for the course. For example, admirable organization or style may differ markedly for a student in a two-year technical program and a student in a four-year school that stresses the arts and humanities.

The following examples of graded papers attempt to put into practice the grading techniques suggested in this chapter. Because of the wide variations one can expect between schools and courses, ranges of quality rather than specific grades are suggested: good, average, and weak. Keep in mind that these are merely samples and that the best grading pro-

cedures are those that reflect the personality of the teacher
as a sensitive and thorough reader:

GOOD

> [Write an essay in which you try to give your
> readers a fresh look at a subject, perhaps by
> choosing one they probably have not paid much
> attention to in the past. You may wish to
> present examples, look at causes and effects,
> classify, or compare and contrast. Remember that
> the detail you use to develop your essay and make
> your point will help determine the essay's
> effectiveness.]

Winter in New England

So you were raised in Miami and now you are
moving to New England. You say you are excited
about the move, but do you know how your life
will change here? Living in a cold climate like
New England's influences how you spend your
money, what you do with your time, and how you
feel about yourself and others.

good. opening paragraph

The most obvious effect of the winter cold
is financial, as you'll quickly learn. Even
though you only wear casual clothes, you'll need
a new wardrobe: a collection of sweaters and
flannel shirts; a very warm coat; and a pair of
boots suitable for deep snow, glassy ice, messy
slush, and rain. You have probably heard enough
about our heating bills up here, so I won't go
into that financial effect of the cold. But you
may not know what this climate will do to your
car. You'll have to "winterize" it, which means
putting antifreeze in the radiator and who knows
what else. Inevitably, more than once your
winterized car will refuse to start in the cold

explaining this a bit more would make your point even more effective.

weather, so you'll have to fork over money for
road service or towing. But that inconvenience
and cost does not compare to the agony of
watching your car disintegrate over a few years
from the salt laid down on roads to melt ice.

yes, this really is agony.

Even if you are prepared for the financial
costs of living in the North, you will probably
be startled by how the cold climate affects your
activities. Winter here is hibernating time.
The outdoors is something to be passed through as
quickly as possible on your way from one heated
place to another. In winter you resign yourself
to huddling around the radiator (if you have paid
the heating bill). With all your money going
toward self-defense from the cold, boredome can
be a problem, so you may find yourself cooking
soups, playing games, or imprinting on the
television. Actually, you may end up relishing
your free time, no matter how boring or
frustrating, when you experience the great winter
activity--battling ice and snow. If it's a wet
winter, count on spending a few hours minimum
every week shoveling snow from driveways and
sidewalks, scraping ice and snow off your car,
and (most fun of all) pushing your car or someone
else's out of icy snowbanks.

sp

this is an interesting use of the word.

Ugh! (but these are good details)

The strangest effect of life in the cold is
the way it influences your attitudes. After a
hot, humid summer the crisp, dry air of autumn at
first fills you with energy and cheerfulness.
But, as the air becomes downright chilly and the
tree brances become bare, you will sense yourself
and others dying a little each day. Gradually you

true - good insight into human nature

73

find it necessary to don heavy, constricting
clothing; you avoid any contact with the depres-
sing out-of-doors; you begin to shiver inside
your own home, for turning on the heat for the
first time since last winter is <u>an admission of</u>
<u>death</u> that everyone puts off. But inevitably *good phrase*
winter comes, in full force. Your face feels
tight, and you see your expression mirrored in
the thin-lipped scowls of the people you pass *excellent detail*
quickly on the street. Your posture is hunched,
elbows squeezed to the waist, and your mood is
similarly withdrawn. Except for the Christmas/
Chanukah frenzy, you will spend the next four
months in a gray mood that matches the dominant
color of the sky.

So you won't be discouraged from coming
north at all, I've held the saving grace of
winter for last. It ends. And when the
punishment finally stops, you understand that you
had to go through it to experience the sheer
elation of spring. So come ahead and do not
fear. Bad as it is, winter is worth the intense
joy of its leaving.

*Fine paper. Your thesis is clear
and you develop each part of it with
effective detail. The third set of effects
you discuss, the effect on feelings,
is particularly insightful. And the
last paragraph ties the whole essay
together nicely.*

AVERAGE

[Assignment: Write an essay in which you use
classification to help readers understand a
complicated topic or to highlight the characteristics of groups of people, ideas, objects,
or events in such a way that you shed fresh light
on the subject. Remember that the details you
use to develop your essay will help determine its
effectiveness.]

THE SECOND HALF OF SLEEPING: WAKING

The human being, it is estimated, sleeps
away one third of his life. Much research on
this topic has been done in sleep clinics
throughout the world. A more fasinating aspect
of the sleeping process has been virtually
ignored: waking up. The ways in which people
wake up can, however, be narrowed down and
described in four main groups.

21j

the thesis is clear, but not very interesting

The Last-Minute Riser is often seen
stumbling through the quad, five minutes into
class time, with wet hair and still wearing
pajamas. The actual waking process is an
extremely painful one. The last minute riser has
mathematically calculated the number of minutes
it takes to get ready in the morning. He is
awakened by the piercing screech of the alarm
clock at the predetermined moment, and again five
minutes later, and five minutes after that.
Alarm clock manufacturers have installed "snooze
buttons" on alarm clocks for people falling into
this category. The last minute riser realizes

17a

hyph

good

hyph

with a mixture of shock and terror that he has
slept well into the alloted getting-ready time.
He begins an <u>emotional display of a person in</u> *w*
panic as he rushes to and fro <u>throughout the</u> *w*
<u>room</u> in an effort to make up for lost time. This
person never has time for breakfast and must deal
with an array of stomach gurgling noises that *hyph*
last through his first three classes. Persons
fitting this description have been known to *true!*
change in and out of majors so as to avoid
required morning classes.

The Early Birds are in direct contrast to
hyph the last minute riser. Early birds are easy to
spot, they are the people who look bright-eyed, *GS*
(22e) and cheerfully well-rested; the people who *¶*
eagerly answer questions during an eight o'clock *dev*
class. They make a point to skip to the
cafeteria every morning to eat an elaborate meal.
Then the early bird is fully alert and anxious to
begin the day.

¶ The Zombie is a living testimonial to the
dev theory that we are fully alert only one minute of
each hour. The zombie is not aware of his alarm
clock when it buzzes, but he manages to shut it
off anyway. A zombie usually awakens half way
through lunch. Although this is a daily
occurence, he is nonetheless always bewildered at

finding that he is not asleep in bed as he
imagined.

true

The Complainer does not enjoy waking up, as
is well known by anyone he lives with. He finds
it soothing to know that although he is unhappily
awake, so, too, is anyone within listening range.
The complainer allows his alarm clock to beep
continuously for twenty minutes. He does not
hear this; everyone else in his dorm does. When

dm he does respond, the alarm clock is hurled across
his room. It lands with a blood-curdling crash.
The complainer is ready to get up. He shocks the
room to life by turning on every light and
      ww (while ?)
blaring his stereo. When attempting to get
ready, the complainer is unable to find any of
his belongings. He finds it necessary to awaken
      sp' no commas necessary
his roomate several times and make him aware of
the dilemma. After slamming shut any drawer
within reach, he stomps to the cafeteria. The
cafeteria is often visited by complainers, as it   *good phrase*
supplies an inexhaustible supply of subjects to
grieve over. It is best to avoid the complainer
until noontime.

In college life, a person is forced to deal
with others every hour of the day: the hours when
others are asleep, awake, and especially the
hours in between. Awareness of the ways different people wake up is necessary if one is to
survive the first half of every day.

This essay is often quite funny, but the paragraphs on "The Early Birds" and "The Zombie" need more development. You might add details like those in the paragraphs describing the other categories. The thesis is clear, but it is not very interesting. You might try to indicate what the reader will learn from your essay -- you do this effectively in the last paragraph. Watch out for the sentence and punctuation problems. Look up the appropriate sections in the <u>Handbook</u>.

WEAK

[Assignment: Write a narrative about an event in your life that had an important impact on you or that you remember vividly because of the insight it gave you into yourself and other people. Remember to choose details carefully because they will play an important role in making your narrative vivid and effective.]

THE FIRST DAY

It was a beautiful day in late August, kind of warm and very nervewracking for me. <u>Because I was embarking on the most important day in my life, the beginning of my college experience.</u> (10a) The day began with its normal rituals and everything appeared to be fine until I arrived at the college. Suddenly I found myself asking, what am I doing here, am I really ready for this. (24a)

I wanted to cry, but I pushed back the tears and
plunged onward. Before I knew it, I was pushed
sp
amoungst the hustle and bustle of the first day.

good   *whose*
I must have looked like a child whoe teddy
bear was taken from him.   *3c*
sp
Being as how I was truely frightened I
sp
desparately tried to find my first class and with
sp
the aide of a few older students I successfully
found my place.
sp
After that things got easier, but not to.
The hardest part was yet to come. The adjustment *10d*
to new and different people. The biggest
difficulty was starting a conversation. Most of
13a the time you say nothing for the fear of sounding
dumb. The first time beginning to talk to
good someone, my voice cracks and I must have turned *t* *dm*
detail scarlet red, but I never stuck around to find
find out what? *sp*
out. I snuck out quicly and found the nearest
(lady's) room. *ladies' (ladies is plural)*

The strange thing about college is its *a professor is a "he" or a "she"*
sp
proffessors. Each has (its) own technique but the
one *s*
same basics. On the first day they each tell you *use the*
he or she *s*   *singular*
what they expect during the semester and then *here*
too much exaggeration here
they hand you a forty page syllabus of work to be
done in fifteen weeks. I had (another) who when *one professor*
3/c
(every time) she spoke sounded like she was having *!!*
her hand for dinner.

this A doesn't fit with the thesis

People asked me what I thought about my
first year in school. My response is simply, "It
was different". *You didn't really cover this much territory in the essay.*

79

This is a good topic for an essay, but you need to spend more time describing specific incidents so that your readers can share and understand your experiences. The second and third paragraphs, for example, are far too short. They ought to be combined and developed with concrete detail. The fourth paragraph also needs to contain specific incidents -- you would be better off concentrating on the first day and describing the events in detail. The paragraph about professors doesn't seem to fit in with the rest of the essay because it covers a different topic.

When you revise, try to focus the essay more clearly on the first day and pay attention to the marginal comments.

EVALUATING FOR REVISION

In recent years the process of revision has come to be viewed as increasingly important in composition instruction. Teachers who make revision a regular part of their composition classes argue that writers should be judged not (or not only) on the basis of the early version of an essay, but also on what they are able to make of the essay by revising it, perhaps taking into account the comments of a sensitive reader.

Composition teachers have, of course, long viewed revision as an important process for student writers to learn. What is new is the extent to which revision is being made a regular part of instruction, an emphasis reflected in its extensive treatment in Chapter 2 of The Little, Brown Handbook.

Many of the techniques already discussed for commenting on papers can be used to aid revision, particularly those that refer students to sections of the Handbook for advice on improving a passage or correcting errors. But evaluation for revision is more likely to suggest extensive changes in a paper, often encouraging the writer to adopt a different perspective on a topic. An instructor might point out, for example, how a paper might be more effective if the writer shifted from an argument about recent government regulations controlling the disposal of dangerous substances to a careful examination of the effects of toxic wastes or to a discussion of the costs for industry of completely safe disposal procedures.

In commenting on papers for revision, you should mark any serious errors but at the same time keep in mind this maxim: "Don't spend time revising a sentence that ought to be dropped from the paper." Remember, too, that awkward and confused sentences are often signs of confusion about the overall direction of an essay and may disappear as the writer resolves the larger problems. Thus comments to aid revision are generally most effective when they are directed both at specific errors and at the larger context, as in this comment: "You shift pronouns often in this passage, sometimes addressing the reader as 'you,' sometimes using 'one' or 'we.' I think the root of the problem is that you are not sure whom you are addressing. Since you are talking about a situation that you face along with most readers, you might choose 'we' and <u>stick to it</u>."

In addition, most students need to know more than what sections of a paper ought to be revised; they need advice about the process of revision itself. By focusing on how to go about revising rather than solely on what changes to make, you can avoid doing the students' work for them. Instead of simply telling a student to add more detail to an essay on the effects of unemployment, you might say, "Imagine that you are the father of five children and that your wife is a homemaker. You have just lost your job. Write for five minutes about how your being home all day, depressed because you are out of work, might upset the normal life of your family. When you are done, look over what you have written for details and examples you can use in your paper." Advice of this sort not only helps a student revise the paper at hand, but it also shows the student ways to revise future papers.

PEER GRADING AND CONFERENCES

Conferences and peer grading are worthwhile alternatives to written responses. While some instructors rely solely on these methods, most use them as supplements to provide a fresh perspective for student writers. Conferences give an instructor a chance to respond to essays as a sensitive reader, with opinions and feelings, words of encouragement, and suggested corrections—all of which are generally hard to convey in the margins of papers. Conferences also require students to contribute by commenting on their own papers, explaining why they made certain choices, and indicating how they want to revise an essay or how they plan to change their approach in the next assignment. In a conference you may find that your judgment of a paper or of the source and seriousness of a writing problem changes when you hear what the student writer was trying to accomplish.

In peer grading, the students form small groups in class, listen to or read their fellow students' papers, and offer comments, encouragement, and criticism. Comments from fellow students can be very effective. Even if the comments are not exactly those the instructor would make, they can be useful (if they are honest) because they give the writer an idea of how a real audience responds to his or her work. But most students are polite; if left on their own to decide what comments to make, they will be as supportive as they can and avoid the kind of negative comments that may be necessary for improvement. In setting up peer-critique or -grading groups, you may have to take a number of steps so that they function effectively.

1. Keep the groups small: Three or four students in each group is ideal. With larger numbers, the group will not have time to go over all the papers in a single class session. Having at least three students in a group means, moreover, that each paper gets at least two responses, each, presumably, with a slightly different perspective.

2. Have students make carbons, dittos, or photocopies of their papers ahead of time so that each member of the group has a copy to read. Reading the papers aloud can help the writer spot problems, but it is still easier for the other students to respond to a paper they have read than one they have heard.

3. When the groups are new, provide students with questions to ask about each paper. Because students have not had much experience as critics, they are more likely to make useful comments if they begin by looking for answers to questions such as "What is the thesis and where is it in the paper?" "Does each paragraph in the body of the paper provide an extended example or abundant details to support the thesis?" "Does the paper contain sentence fragments or problems in agreement?"

4. Asking the students to paraphrase a paper can help them spot problems and strengths. A student can begin a response by saying, "I thought _____ was the point you were trying to make in this essay. Am I right?" If the point is clear, then the writer will know he or she has done an effective piece of writ-

ing; if it is not clear, the writer will be aware of the problem.

5. Let the students know that the harder they work in the groups the more their writing is likely to improve. Leave them alone for a while; but check up on the work of each group by the end of the class session.

Peer critiques will not solve all of the students' writing problems, but they can provide motivation and a sense of audience, two elements essential for improvement in writing. At their best, too, they can provide valuable advice for beginning writers, advice that students are generally quite willing to listen to.

Chapter 4

TEACHING COMPOSITION: A SELECTIVE BIBLIOGRAPHY

During the last two decades, a great deal has been written about the teaching of composition, from both theoretical and practical perspectives. This bibliography is designed as a selective guide to the resources available to composition teachers. It opens with general works on composition, then lists books and articles on the major topics covered by The Little, Brown Handbook, and concludes by reviewing materials in areas of special interest to composition teachers:

General Works
        Teaching Composition
        Theoretical Background
The Whole Paper and Paragraphs
        Developing an Essay: Aims and Modes
        Developing an Essay: Getting Ideas and
                              Developing the Thesis
        Developing an Essay: Considering an Audience
        Developing an Essay: Organizing
        Writing and Revising the Essay
        Composing Good Paragraphs
        Convincing a Reader
Sentences
        Grammatical Sentences
        Clear Sentences
        Effective Sentences
Words, Punctuation, and Mechanics
        Punctuation/Mechanics
        Effective Words
        Spelling
Special Writing Assignments
        The Research Paper
        Practical Writing
Evaluation/Peer Grading
Sentence Combining
Setting Up a Writing Lab

The bibliography is selective in three ways. The emphasis throughout is on articles and books with a practical aim and theoretical works with direct practical applications.

Works with implications for all levels, whatever their
original focus--basic, regular, or advanced composition--have
generally been chosen over works with a narrower focus. And
in an attempt to balance the coverage of different topics,
entries have been limited in areas about which a good deal
has been written--invention and paragraphing, for example--
even at the expense of excluding some well-known items.
(Many of the better-known items are reprinted in the various
collections listed in the bibliography, however.)
      The number of journals publishing articles in rhetoric
and composition has also grown rapidly in recent years. The
following journals regularly contain discussions of interest
to composition teachers and are available in many depart-
mental or college libraries (abbreviations given below are
used throughout the bibliography):

> College Composition and Communication (CCC)
> College English (CE)
> Freshman English News (FEN)
> Journal of Basic Writing (JBW)
> English Journal
> Research in the Teaching of English
> Rhetoric Society Quarterly
> The English Record
> Exercise Exchange
> Teaching English in the Two-Year College
> Improving College and University Teaching

Some other, newer journals in the field include The Writing
Teacher (Freshman Writing Program, University of Southern
California), Writing Lab Newsletter (Writing Lab, Purdue
University), and The Writing Center Journal (English Depart-
ment, State University of New York at Albany).
      In addition, the National Council of Teachers of English
(NCTE) publishes a wide range of monographs, collections of
essays, and books useful to writing teachers. These are
listed in an annual catalog, Professional Publications for
the Teacher of English and Language Arts, available from
National Council of Teachers of English, 1111 Kenyon Road,
Urbana, IL 61801. Many state and regional affiliates of NCTE
also publish journals (e.g., Illinois English Bulletin,
Connecticut English Journal).
      NCTE publishes annually a volume of essays in the series
"Classroom Practices in Teaching English." The following
volumes are cited frequently (by title) in this bibliography:

> On Righting Writing. Ed. Ouida H. Clapp. Urbana, Ill.:
>   NCTE, 1975.

Teaching the Basics--Really! Ed. Ouida Clapp. Urbana,
    Ill.: NCTE, 1977.
Activating the Passive Student. Ed. Gene Stanford. Ur-
    bana, Ill.: NCTE, 1978.
How to Handle the Paper Load. Ed. Gene Stanford.
    Urbana, Ill.: NCTE, 1979.
Structuring for Success in the English Classroom. Ed.
    Candy Carter. Urbana, Ill.: NCTE, 1982.

Many essays listed in the bibliography are reprinted in the
following collection of some of the best recent articles in
rhetoric and composition (cited as Tate and Corbett):

    Tate, Gary, and Edward P. J. Corbett, eds. The Writing
        Teacher's Sourcebook. New York: Oxford Univ.
        Press, 1981.

GENERAL WORKS

Teaching Composition

Berthoff, Ann E. The Making of Meaning: Metaphors, Models,
    Maxims for Writing Teachers. Montclair, N.J.: Boynton/
    Cook, 1981. Essays on the formative power of language
    and its role in the teaching of writing.
CCCC Committee on Teaching and Its Evaluation in Composi-
    tion. "Evaluating Instruction in Writing: Approaches
    and Instruments." CCC, 33 (May 1982), 213-29. Ques-
    tionnaires that can help describe and evaluate compo-
    sition programs, teachers' attitudes, classroom ac-
    tivities, commentary on student papers, and students'
    judgments of courses and teachers.
Donovan, Timothy R., and Ben W. McClelland, eds. Eight
    Approaches to Teaching Composition. Urbana, Ill.:
    NCTE, 1980. Essays describing a variety of approaches
    to teaching writing: rhetorical, experiential, epi-
    stemic, basic, conferencing, prose models, process, and
    cross-disciplinary.
Irmscher, William F. Teaching Expository Writing. New York:
    Holt, 1979. Introduction to the teaching of writing:
    planning a course, making assignments, teaching struc-
    ture and style, and evaluating papers.
Lindemann, Erika. A Rhetoric for Writing Teachers. New
    York: Oxford Univ. Press, 1982. Survey of contemporary
    rhetorical theory and teaching strategies.
Neman, Beth. Teaching Students to Write. Columbus, Ohio:
    Merrill, 1980. Advice for teaching expository and

creative writing; emphasizes thesis and outlining;
discusses dialects and sentence combining.

Ohmann, Richard, and W. B. Coley, eds. Ideas for English
101: Teaching Writing in College. Urbana, Ill.: NCTE,
1975. Articles from College English, 1966-75. Discussions of teaching methods and class activities.

Shaughnessey, Mina P. Errors and Expectations: A Guide for
the Teacher of Basic Writing. New York: Oxford Univ.
Press, 1977. Focuses on basic writing, but an important
work for teachers of writing at all levels. Detailed
analysis of the causes of student errors; useful strategies for dealing with writing problems.

Tibbetts, Arnold M. Working Papers: A Teacher's Observations
on Composition. Chicago: Scott, Foresman, 1982.
Practical advice for teaching sentences, paragraphs,
organization, stance, and argument.

Wiener, Harvey S. The Writing Room: A Resource Book for
Teachers of English. New York: Oxford Univ. Press,
1981. Advice for the teacher of basic writing:
activities, assignments, and course designs. Comprehensive bibliography.

Theoretical Background

Bartholomae, David. "The Study of Error." CCC, 31 (October
1980), 253-69. Reports that having basic writers read
their papers aloud helps identify sources of error and
can help improve writing.

Britton, James, et al. The Development of Writing Abilities
(11-18). London: Macmillan, 1975. Examines student
writing within a comprehensive framework of audiences
and functions.

Cooper, Charles R., and Lee Odell. Research on Composing:
Points of Departure. Urbana, Ill.: NCTE, 1978.
Collection of essays reviewing recent scholarship and
pointing out directions for future research.

Dillon, George L. Constructing Texts: Elements of a Theory
of Composition and Style. Bloomington, Ind.: Indiana
Univ. Press, 1981. Suggests that teachers adopt the
perspective of current reading theory, which assigns the
reader a role in constructing the meaning of a text.

Emig, Janet. The Composing Processes of Twelfth Graders.
Urbana, Ill.: NCTE, 1971. The first important study of
the composing process; based on case studies. Upsets
some traditional assumptions about prewriting and offers
useful general schema of the process.

----------. "Writing as a Mode of Learning." CCC, 28 (May
1977), 122-28. (Tate and Corbett, pp. 69-78.) Writing

is an intellectual and formative activity, valuable beyond its use in communicating and persuading.

Hirsch, E. D., Jr. The Philosophy of Composition. Chicago: Univ. of Chicago Press, 1977. Important for its defense of the teaching of standard English and for "readability" as the primary criterion for evaluation.

Mailloux, Steven. "Literary Criticism and Composition Theory." CCC, 29 (October 1978), 267-71. Draws parallels between current composition theory and contemporary literary theory, particularly reader-response criticism.

Moffett, James. Teaching the Universe of Discourse. Boston: Houghton Mifflin, 1968. Presents a coherent and extensive program of discourse education, based partly on Piaget's theories of language development.

Smith, Frank. Writing and the Writer. New York: Holt, 1982. Psycholinguistic view of the relationships among writing, thinking, and reading.

Tate, Gary, ed. Teaching Composition: Ten Bibliographical Essays. Fort Worth: Texas Christian Univ. Press, 1976. Review essays on invention, structure, modes, style, dialects, and related areas of interest to composition teachers.

Winterowd, W. Ross, ed. Contemporary Rhetoric: A Conceptual Background with Readings. New York: Harcourt, 1975. Collection of articles on invention, form, and style, with introductions by the editor.

Woodson, Linda. A Handbook of Modern Rhetorical Terms. Urbana, Ill.: NCTE, 1979. Concise, useful definitions.

Young, Richard. "Concepts of Art and the Teaching of Writing." In The Rhetorical Tradition and Modern Writing. Ed. James J. Murphy. New York: Modern Language Association, 1982, pp. 130-41. Argues that current approaches to composition treat the process of discovery in two different ways: by introducing heuristic procedures to guide discovery and by devising situations to encourage creativity.

Young, Richard E., Alton L. Becker, and Kenneth L. Pike. Rhetoric: Discovery and Change. New York: Harcourt, 1970. Applies tagmemic theory to rhetoric; considered one of the most important works of the last two decades. For a briefer treatment see Richard E. Young and Alton L. Becker, "Toward a Modern Theory of Rhetoric: A Tagmemic Contribution," Harvard Educational Review, 35 (Fall 1965), 450-68. (Tate and Corbett, pp. 129-48.)

THE WHOLE PAPER AND PARAGRAPHS

Developing an Essay: Aims and Modes

Connors, Robert J. "The Rise and Fall of the Modes of Discourse." CCC, 32 (December 1981), 444-55. Traces the
rise of the traditional modes (narration, description,
exposition, and argument) in nineteenth-century rhetoric, their dominance in textbooks during the first half
of this century, and their loss of influence during the
last two decades.

Corbett, Edward P. J. Classical Rhetoric for the Modern
Student. 2nd ed. New York: Oxford Univ. Press, 1972.
A textbook that is the best attempt to adapt classical
rhetoric to the modern composition classroom.

D'Angelo, Frank. A Conceptual Theory of Rhetoric. Boston:
Little, Brown, 1975. Argues that rhetorical patterns
of organization (e.g., analysis, classification, description) are also patterns of thought and invention
and can be used to probe experience as part of the composing process. See also "Paradigms as Structural
Counterparts of Topoi," in Linguistics, Stylistics, and
the Teaching of Composition, ed. Donald McQuade (Akron,
Ohio: L&S Books, Univ. of Akron, 1979), pp. 41-51, and a
textbook, Process and Thought in Composition (Boston:
Little, Brown, 1980).

Eckhardt, Caroline D., and David H. Stewart. "Towards a
Functional Taxonomy of Composition." CCC, 30 (December
1979), 338-42. (Tate and Corbett, pp. 100-06.) Classifies writing according to four basic purposes: to
clarify, to substantiate, to evaluate, or to recommend.

Kinneavy, James L. A Theory of Discourse. Englewood Cliffs,
N.J.: Prentice-Hall, 1971. Classifies kinds of discourse according to purpose and emphasis. Expressive
discourse emphasizes the writer or speaker; persuasive
discourse focuses on the audience; referential discourse
focuses on the subject and may be informative, scientif-
ic, or exploratory; and literary discourse emphasizes
the text.

Knoblauch, C. H. "Intentionality in the Writing Process: A
Case Study." CCC, 31 (May 1980), 153-59. Argues that
the purposes used to classify finished works differ from
the "operational" purposes that guide the act of writing and suggests that the teacher of composition needs
to pay attention to the shifting, tentative purposes
that guide writing.

Developing an Essay: Getting Ideas and Developing the Thesis

No area of composition research has received more
attention in recent years than the process of finding
materials for an essay, focusing the topic, and developing a
stance (thesis). The works cited below call attention to
some of the most widely accepted teaching strategies,
including freewriting and question systems (heuristics).
Other resources are described by David V. Harrington et al.,
"A Critical Survey of Resources for Teaching Rhetorical
Invention: A Review-Essay," CE, 40 (February 1979), 641-61.
(Tate and Corbett, pp. 187-206.)

Coe, Richard M. "If Not to Narrow, Then How to Focus: Two
    Techniques for Focusing." CCC, 31 (October 1981), 272-
    77. Ways to get students to focus on a particular
    aspect of a topic as an alternative to the usual
    approach of narrowing a topic.
Comprone, Joseph. "Using Film Within the Composing Process."
    FEN, 10 (Spring 1981), 21-24. Demonstrates how contem-
    porary heuristics and problem-solving techniques can be
    used to probe initial responses to a film and generate
    form in the different stages of writing; includes sum-
    mary of an appropriate short film.
Denman, Mary Edel. "I Got This Here Hang-Up: Non-Cognitive
    Processes for Facilitating Writing." CCC, 26 (1975),
    305-09. Activities and paper assignments designed to
    help students overcome anxiety about writing.
Flinn, Jane Zeni. "Journals: Write More--Grade Less." In
    How to Handle the Paper Load, pp. 9-14. Suggests using
    student journals to develop ideas for a wide variety of
    writing assignments including description, autobiog-
    raphy, research writing, analysis, and persuasion.
Flower, Linda S., and John R. Hayes. "Problem-Solving Strat-
    egies and the Writing Process." CE, 39 (December
    1977), 442-48. Techniques for discovering and devel-
    oping ideas, including cue words, nutshelling, idea
    trees, role playing, and brainstorming.
Fulwiler, Toby E. "Journal Writing Across the Curriculum."
    In How to Handle the Paper Load, pp. 15-22. Describes
    ways to use journals as part of the learning process in
    classes in all disciplines--for in-class writing,
    problem solving, homework, and record keeping.
King, Barbara. "The Waiting Game: Structuring the English
    Class for Prewriting." In Structuring for Success in
    the English Classroom, pp. 83-87. Prewriting activities
    that can take place in class.
Kneupper, Charles W. "Revising the Tagmemic Heuristic:
    Theoretical and Pedagogical Considerations." CCC, 31

(May 1980), 160–68. A simplified version of the question system introduced by Young, Becker, and Pike in Rhetoric: Discovery and Change (see above, "General Works: Theoretical Background").

Larson, Richard. "Problem-Solving, Composing and Liberal Education." CE, 33 (March 1972), 628–35. A stimulating application of a problem-solving model to some aspects of rhetorical invention.

Odell, Lee. "Teaching Writing by Teaching the Process of Discovery: An Interdisciplinary Enterprise." In Cognitive Processes in Writing. Ed. Lee W. Gregg and Erwin Steinberg. Hillsdale, N.J.: Lawrence Erlbaum Associates, 1980, pp. 139–54. Using writing assignments to help students ask questions about a subject and encourage insight and discovery. Presents an extended example using Hersey's Hiroshima.

Price, Gayle B. "A Case for a Modern Commonplace Book." CCC, 31 (May 1980), 175–82. Reviews freewriting and other techniques for helping students generate ideas and tells how students can record ideas for writing in a notebook.

Rodrigues, Raymond J. "Folklife: An Unlimited Writing Source." In On Righting Writing, pp. 37–39. List of family and community traditions students can explore as sources for essays.

Rohman, D. Gordon. "Pre-Writing: The State of Discovery in the Writing Process." CCC, 16 (May 1965), 106–12. A program of invention based on techniques of self-analysis and meditation. Emphasis on writing as a self-actualizing process.

Selfe, Cynthia L., and Sue Rodi. "An Invention Heuristic for Expressive Writing." CCC, 31 (May 1980), 169–74. Questions students can use to gain personal insight and to help produce good expressive writing.

Washington, Eugene. "WH-Questions in Teaching Composition." CCC, 28 (February 1977), 54–56. Using what, why, where, and how questions to increase density of information in essays and clarify structure.

Wilson, Dawn W. "Steppingstones to Success: A Journal-Based Composition Course." In Structuring for Success in the English Classroom, pp. 67–72. Using journal entries to probe subjects and as the basis of different kinds of papers throughout the course.

Developing an Essay: Considering an Audience

Baldwin, Dean R. "Introducing Rhetoric in Remedial Writing-Courses." CCC, 29 (December 1978), 392–94.

Prewriting sheets to help students identify an occasion, audience, and purpose for their writing.

Davis, Ken. "The Circle Game: A Heuristic for Discovering Rhetorical Situations." CCC, 29 (October 1978), 285-87. Suggests giving students roles to play in social situations and challenging them to develop writing tasks appropriate to the situations.

Flower, Linda S., and John R. Hayes. "The Cognition of Discovery: Defining a Rhetorical Problem." CCC, 31 (February 1980), 21-32. Detailed study of how good and poor writers conceive of writing tasks as they begin to compose.

Long, Russell C. "Writer-Audience Relationships: Analysis or Invention?" CCC, 31 (May 1980), 221-26. Kinds of strategies student writers must develop to create in their minds the potential audiences for their writing.

Ong, Walter J., S.J. "The Writer's Audience Is Always a Fiction." PMLA, 90 (January 1975), 9-21. Argues that writers must construct audiences in their imaginations as an essential part of the act of writing and that readers must play the role defined for them by the writer's act of imagination.

Pfister, Fred R., and Joan Petrick. "A Heuristic Model for Creating a Writer's Audience." CCC, 31 (May 1980), 213-20. Questions writers can ask to probe the nature of a potential audience and the relationships among the audience, the subject, the writer, and possible forms of expression.

Tedlock, David. "The Case Approach to Composition." CCC, 32 (October 1981), 253-61. Suggests using detailed, self-contained descriptions of a writing situation, "cases," as a basis for assignments and instruction.

Developing an Essay: Organizing

Berman, Neil. "Language, Process, and Tinkertoys." CCC, 26 (December 1975), 390-92. Using concrete exercises to teach process writing.

Dean, Terry. "Causal, Not Casual: An Advance Organizer for Cause-and-Effect Compositions." In Structuring for Success in the English Classroom, pp. 92-97. Exercises to make students aware of causal relationships and to provide a basis for writing.

Green, Lawrence D. "Enthymemic Invention and Structural Prediction." CE, 41 (February 1980), 623-34. Different kinds of logical strategies and their value in helping structure argumentative essays.

Haich, George D. "If the Reader Never Saw One, How Would You Describe It." CCC, 26 (October 1975), 298-300. Suggests having students describe an object the class has not seen so the class can begin to understand what information and strategies are necessary for effective description.

Hartwell, Patrick. "Teaching Arrangement: A Pedagogy." CE, 40 (January 1979), 548-54. A program where students move from understanding relationships between statements, to understanding relationships among sentences in a paragraph, to understanding larger patterns of organization.

Holloway, Karla F. C. "Teaching Composition Through Outlining." In Teaching the Basics--Really! pp. 36-39. Using outlines as a critical tool to teach writing.

Larson, Richard L. "Towards a Linear Rhetoric of the Essay." CCC, 22 (May 1971), 140-46. Proposes teaching students to shape their essays by planning a linear sequence of moves or stages rather than a hierarchical structure.

Podis, Leonard A. "Teaching Arrangement: Defining a More Practical Approach." CCC, 31 (May 1980), 197-204. Proposes a teaching sequence designed to make students aware of the basic principles of organization; reviews some standard patterns of arrangement useful for academic and professional writing.

Stitzel, Judith G. "'Is There a Box on the Board?' An Exercise in Classification." In On Righting Writing, pp. 87-93. Classroom activities providing an awareness of how the mind organizes perceptions, ideas, and experience.

Writing and Revising the Essay

Bruffee, Kenneth. "Getting Started." In Linguistics, Stylistics, and the Teaching of Composition. Ed. Donald McQuade. Akron, Ohio: L&S Books, Univ. of Akron, 1979, pp. 52-60. Problems on the sentence level and in the essay as a whole viewed as the result of confusion about where the essay is going.

Butturff, Douglas R., and Nancy I. Sommers. "Placing Revision in a Reinvented Rhetorical Tradition." In Reinventing the Rhetorical Tradition. Ed. Aviva Freedman and Ian Pringle. Conway, Ark.: L&S Books, Univ. of Central Arkansas, 1980, pp. 99-104. Argues that comments on papers should help students learn writing procedures that will enable them to make effective revisions.

Coe, Richard M., and Kris D. Gutierrez. "Using Problem-Solving Procedures and Process Analysis to Help Students with Writing Problems." CCC, 32 (October 1981), 262-71. Assignments and activities designed to make students aware of how they go about writing, to help them understand their strengths and weaknesses as writers, and to give them greater control over their composing processes.

Elbow, Peter. Writing with Power: Techniques for Mastering the Writing Process. New York: Oxford Univ. Press, 1981. Techniques for effective writing and revising, including dealing with audience and feedback.

----------. Writing Without Teachers. New York: Oxford Univ. Press, 1973. Freewriting and other techniques for tapping imagination and creativity during the writing process.

Flower, Linda. "Writer-Based Prose: A Cognitive Basis for Problems in Writing." CE, 41 (September 1979), 19-37. (Tate and Corbett, pp. 268-92.) Argues that writers must learn to transform what they have to say from the form in which they have come to understand it (writer-based prose) to the form in which readers can understand it (reader-based prose.).

Flower, Linda, and John R. Hayes. "A Cognitive Process Theory of Writing." CCC, 32 (December 1981), 365-87. Presents a model of composing that highlights the elements of the process and the goals that guide it.

Koch, Carl, and James M. Brazil. Strategies for Teaching the Composition Process. Urbana, Ill.: NCTE, 1978. Exercises and activities for all stages of writing.

Lamberg, Walter J. "Following a Short Narrative Through the Composing Process." In Teaching the Basics--Really! pp. 30-35. Suggests that introducing students to the composing process must involve analyzing the writing task, getting feedback, using models, and repeating the task.

Larsen, Richard B. "Back to the Board." CCC, 29 (October 1978) 292-94. Instructor writes an essay on the board while students write in class.

Shuman, R. Baird. "Basics in Composition: Fluency First." In Teaching the Basics--Really! pp. 43-46. Activities to overcome the fear of writing and help students get started.

Sommers, Nancy. "Revision Strategies of Student Writers and Experienced Adult Writers." CCC, 31 (December 1980), 378-88. Students see revision as changes in small units--words and sentences; experienced writers see it as a recursive process directed at larger units of the text and the meaning it conveys.

Southwell, Michael G. "Free Writing in Composition Classes."
CE, 38 (March 1977), 676-81. Freewriting to encourage
fluent writing and provide material that can be used for
working on basic skills or as a preparation for more
formal papers.

Wason, P. C. "Specific Thoughts on the Writing Process." In
Cognitive Processes in Writing. Ed. Lee W. Gregg and
Erwin R. Steinberg. Hillsdale, N.J.: Lawrence Erlbaum
Associates, 1980, pp. 129-37. Multiple drafts often
necessary because writing consists of two processes hard
to undertake at the same time: saying (or discovering)
something and saying it correctly.

Composing Good Paragraphs

Becker, A. L. "A Tagmemic Approach to Paragraph Analysis."
CCC, 16 (December 1965), 237-42. Observes that expository paragraphs generally follow a variation of one of
two patterns: topic-restriction-illustration (TRI) or
problem-solution (PS).

Brostoff, Anita. "Coherence: 'Next to' Is Not 'Connected
To.'" CCC, 32 (October 1981), 278-94. Discusses the
causes of lack of coherence in writing and describes a
program for helping students achieve coherence.

Christensen, Francis. "A Generative Rhetoric of the Paragraph." In Notes Towards a New Rhetoric: Nine Essays
for Teachers. Ed. Francis Christensen and Bonniejean
Christensen. 2nd ed. New York: Harper & Row, 1978,
pp. 74-103. Views paragraphs as a series of statements
at differing levels of generality, often moving from the
more general toward the specific.

Clark, Beverly Lyon. "Ranking Writing." In Structuring for
Success in the English Classroom, pp. 126-28. Sample
paragraphs for students to rank and use as a basis for
discussion.

Cohan, Carol. "Writing Effective Paragraphs," CCC, 27
(December 1976), 363-65. Suggests treating topic sentences as questions to be answered by the paragraph that
follows as a way of encouraging paragraph development.

Stern, Arthur A. "When Is a Paragraph?" CCC, 27 (October
1976), 253-57. (Tate and Corbett, pp. 294-300.)
Reviews recent discussions of the paragraph, concluding
that the paragraph is not necessarily a logical pattern
with a clear topic sentence but is instead a flexible
rhetorical structure that can serve a variety of
purposes.

Wiener, Harvey S. "The Single Narrative Paragraph and
College Remediation." CE, 33 (March 1972), 660-69.
Using paragraph-length narrative themes can help
students develop both paragraph and essay skills.
Winterowd, W. Ross. "The Grammar of Coherence." CE, 31
(May 1970), 828-35. (Tate and Corbett, pp. 301-09.)
An attempt to describe the kinds of relations that link
sentence to sentence and paragraph to paragraph.

Convincing a Reader

Crabbe, Katharyn. "Debate/Write: An Approach to Writing
Arguments." CCC, 27 (October 1976), 291-93. Pairing
students for discussion/debate about issues to provide
a way to move from personal to persuasive writing.
Deane, Barbara. "Putting the Inferential Process to Work in
the Classroom." CCC, 27 (February 1976), 50-52. Activities to help students develop their ability to make
accurate inferences.
Katula, Richard A., and Richard W. Roth. "A Stock Issues
Approach to Writing Arguments." CCC, 31 (May 1980),
183-96. A logical and practical system for inventing
and structuring arguments using the points of con-
flict that arise in trying to convince an audience of
a particular solution to a problem.
Kneupper, Charles W. "Teaching Argument: An Introduction to
the Toulmin Model." CCC, 29 (October 1978), 237-41.
Brief review of Stephen Toulmin's simplified, practical
logic, a system based primarily on three elements:
data, claim, and warrant.
Ladd, Rosalind Ekman. "Rational Persuasion: A Philosopher's
Approach to Teaching Writing." The English Record, 33
(Spring 1982), 4-5. Requires students to analyze the
elements of an argument in newspaper writing, present
and respond to oral arguments, and write a term paper
defending a thesis.
Levin, Gerald. "On Freshman Composition and Logical
Thinking." CCC, 28 (December 1977), 359-64. Using
essays on controversial topics as a basis for class
discussion of the features and patterns of argument.
Winder, Barbara E. "The Delineation of Values in Persuasive
Writing." CCC, 29 (February 1978), 55-58. Asks writers
to spell out both sides of an argument to make them sensitive to their own values and those of their readers.

97

SENTENCES

Grammatical Sentences

D'Eloia, Sarah. "The Uses--and Limits--of Grammar." _JBW_,
1 (Spring/Summer 1977), 1-20. (Tate and Corbett, pp.
225-43.) The kinds of errors commonly made by basic-
writing students; includes exercises designed to help
them overcome the errors.

Elgin, Suzette Haden. "Don't No Revolutions Hardly _Ever_ Come
by Here." _CE_, 39 (March 1978), 784-89. Students distinguish acceptable from unacceptable sentences and
write rules to explain the grammatical features illustrated by the sentences.

Freeman, Donald C. "Linguistics and Error Analysis: On
Agency." In _Linguistics, Stylistics, and the Teaching
of Composition_. Ed. Donald McQuade. Akron, Ohio: L&S
Books, Univ. of Akron, 1979, pp. 143-50. Sees many
sentence errors as the result of problems with agency, a
lack of clarity about the person or thing responsible
for the activity presented in the sentence.

Gliserman, Martin. "An Act of Theft: Teaching Grammar."
_CE_, 39 (March 1978), 791-99. Suggests problem-solving
exercises, worksheets, and grammatical poetry as a way
of teaching grammar.

Gorrell, Donna. "Controlled Composition for Basic Writers."
CCC, 32 (October 1981), 308-16. Students manipulate
and alter previously written material to develop basic
skills.

Hays, Janice N. "Teaching the Grammar of Discourse." In
Reinventing the Rhetorical Tradition. Ed. Aviva Freedman and Ian Pringle. Conway, Ark.: L&S Books, Univ. of
Central Arkansas, 1980, pp. 145-55. Exercises to teach
the basic strategies of sentences.

Laurence, Patricia. "Error's Endless Train: Why Students
Don't Perceive Errors." _JBW_, 1 (Spring 1975), 23-42.
Discusses why students do not perceive errors and presents exercises to make students aware of inflections
and easily confused words.

Lunsford, Andrea A. "Cognitive Development and the Basic
Writer." _CE_, 41 (September 1979), 39-46. (Tate
and Corbett, pp. 257-67.) Exercises and assignments
adapted to the cognitive level of basic writers;
designed to help students identify sentence parts and
functions and write sentences using a number of basic
patterns.

Meyers, Lewis. "Teaching Verb Tenses with Pictures." _Exer-
cise Exchange_, 25 (Fall 1980), 6-7. Pictures that pre-

sent events in different time frames as a basis for
oral exercises and writing.

Solomon, Martha. "Teaching the Nominative Absolute." CCC,
26 (December 1975), 356-61. Advice on analyzing and
teaching the absolute.

Sternglass, Marilyn S. "Composition Teacher as Reading
Teacher." CCC, 27 (December 1976), 378-82. Analytical
reading as a way to understand the varieties of basic
sentence structure.

Clear Sentences

Allen, Walter P. "Using Word Groups in Correcting Compositions." CCC, 26 (December 1975), 379-83. Breaking
sentences into word clusters as a way to help students
understand structure and spot and correct errors.

Bamberg, Betty. "Periods Are Basic: A Strategy for Elim-
inating Comma Faults and Run-On Sentences." In Teaching
the Basics—Really! pp. 97-99. Uses oral reading to
identify and correct problems with writing.

Carkeet, David. "Understanding Syntatic Errors in Remedial
Writing." CE, 38 (March 1977), 682-86, 695. Analyzes
kinds of errors frequently made by students and suggests
a model of how to make sympathetic responses.

Chaika, Elaine. "Grammars and Teaching." CE, 39 (March
1978), 770-83. Offers fresh explanations from a
linguistic perspective for a number of standard errors,
including dangling modifiers.

——————. "Who Can Be Taught." CE, 35 (February
1974), 575-83. Suggests that teaching the relationships
that characterize core sentences can help resolve
problems in more complicated sentences.

Harris, Muriel. "Mending the Fragmented Free Modifier."
CCC, 32 (May 1981), 175-82. Strategies for identifying
kinds of fragments and correcting them.

Kline, Charles R., Jr., and W. Dean Memering. "Formal Fragments: The English Minor Sentence." Research in the
Teaching of English, 11 (Fall 1977), 97-110. Identifies
kinds of fragments (minor sentences) often used and
considered acceptable in formal writing.

Krishna, Valerie. "The Syntax of Error." JBW, 1 (Spring
1975), 43-49. Views problems like mixed constructions
and shifts as the result of a weak sentence core, and
encourages teachers to pay attention to this underlying
problem in helping students avoid such errors.

Pixton, William H. "The Dangling Gerund: A Working
Definition." CCC, 24 (May 1973), 193-99. Reviews dis-

cussions of dangling modifiers and, using a variety of sample sentences, formulates a definition of the dangling gerund.

Effective Sentences

Brooks, Phyllis. "Mimesis: Grammar and the Echoing Voice." CE, 35 (November 1973), 161–68. Paraphrases that ask students to imitate the style of a writer but to use a different content; students learn to use a variety of structures including parenthetical expressions, apposition and modification, and parallelism plus reference.

Christensen, Francis. "A Generative Rhetoric of the Sentence." In Notes Towards a New Rhetoric: Nine Essays for Techers. Ed. Francis Christensen and Bonniejean Christensen. 2nd ed. New York: Harper & Row, 1978, 23–44. (Tate and Corbett, pp. 353–67.) Demonstrates how to analyze the levels of generality in sentences and discusses and illustrates the structure of the cumulative sentence.

de Beaugrande, Robert. "Generative Stylistics: Between Grammar and Rhetoric." CCC, 28 (October 1977), 240–46. Argues that sentence emphasis must take into account the relationship of old and new information.

Melamed, Evelyn B., and Harvey Minkoff. "Transitions: A Key to Mature Reading and Writing." In Teaching the Basics Really! pp. 17–21. Exercises to help students make logical links between sentences and parts of sentences with transitions.

Vande Kopple, William J. "Functional Sentence Perspective, Composition, and Reading." CCC, 33 (February 1982), 50–63. Views the relationship of old and new information in sentences and paragraphs as important to comprehension and argues that it should affect the stylistic choices students make.

Walker, Robert L., O.P. "The Common Writer: A Case for Parallel Structure." CCC, 21 (December 1970), 373–79. Believes students should be encouraged to use a variety of sentence structures and be made aware of the need for parallelism, an important feature of mature sentences.

Weathers, Winston. An Alternate Style: Options in Composition. Rochelle Park, N.J.: Hayden, 1980. Imaginative alternatives to the plain style usually emphasized in composition courses.

Williams, Joseph M. Style: Ten Lessons in Clarity and Grace. Glenview, Ill.: Scott, Foresman, 1981. Fresh approaches to achieving clarity in complex writing; discusses the structure of complicated sentences and ways to improve the style of academic and technical prose. A textbook with broad theoretical and practical implications.

WORDS, PUNCTUATION, AND MECHANICS

Punctuation/Mechanics

Benson, S. Kenneth. "Profitable Proofreading." In Teaching the Basics--Really! pp. 80-81. Exercises in proofreading and in getting students to pay attention to correction symbols.

Christensen, Francis. "Restrictive and Nonrestrictive Modifiers Again." In Notes Towards a New Rhetoric: Nine Essays for Teachers. Ed. Francis Christensen and Bonniejean Christensen. 2nd ed. New York: Harper & Row, 1978, pp. 117-32. Discusses and illustrates uses of the comma with a variety of modifying elements.

Collignon, Joseph. "Why Leroy Can't Write." CE, 39 (March 1978), 852-59. Oral reading to help students punctuate correctly and to provide them with models for writing.

Hall, Janice K. "Tackle the Troublespots." In Evaluating and Improving Written Expression: A Practical Guide for Teachers. Boston: Allyn and Bacon, 1981, pp. 153-85. Divides punctuation and mechanical skills into three levels--basic, average, and advanced--and provides numerous activities to teach punctuation, mechanics, and spelling.

Effective Words

Ammirati, Theresa, and Ellen Strenski. "Using Astrology to Teach Connotation and Bias." Exercise Exchange, 25 (Fall 1980), 9-11. Use the language in astrology books as a source of examples of connotation and bias.

Hoover, Regina M. "In the Beginning: The Word." JBW, 2 (Fall/Winter 1979), 82-87. Copying sentences containing unfamiliar words to help build vocabulary and improve writing.

Journal of Basic Writing, 2 (Fall/Winter 1979). Special issue on vocabulary; includes general articles and notes on specific strategies (see both Hoover and Stotsky).

Nilsen, Don L. F. "Clichés, Trite Sayings, Dead Metaphors, and Stale Figures of Speech in Composition Instruction." CCC, 27 (October 1976), 278-82. Reviving dead metaphors

and cliches in class discussion to create an awareness
of figurative language.

Simpson, Mary Scott. "Teaching Writing: Beginning with the
Word." CE, 39 (April 1978), 934-39. Class activities
and readings to develop sensitivity to words and to
build vocabulary.

Sossaman, Stephen. "Detroit Designers: A Game to Teach
Metaphors." Exercise Exchange, 21 (Fall 1976), 2-3.
Car names as good examples of metaphoric language.

Stotsky, Sandra. "Teaching the Vocabulary of Academic
Discourse." JBW, 2 (Fall/Winter 1979), 15-39. Examines the language of textbooks and suggests using reading, dictating, precis writing, and affix study to
develop vocabulary for academic reading and writing.

Spelling

Buck, Jean L. "A New Look at Teaching Spelling." CE, 38
(March 1977), 703-06. Personal word lists drawn from
students' writing as a basis for class activities
including an exchange of lists.

Gere, Ann Ruggles. "Alternatives to Tradition in Teaching
Spelling." In Teaching the Basics--Really! pp. 100-
03. Suggests using individualized word lists and
classroom games and also teaching phoneme-grapheme
correspondences and word division.

Harris, Muriel. "The Big Five: Individualizing Improvement
in Spelling." In Teaching the Basics--Really! pp. 104-
07. Suggests making students aware of their habitual
problems deriving from homophones, pronunciation,
doubled consonants, word roots, and the schwa.

McClellan, Jane. "A Clinic for Misspellers." CE, 40 (November 1978), 324-29. Using several kinds of word lists
and frequent drill to bring about improvement.

SPECIAL WRITING ASSIGNMENTS

The Research Paper

Carpenter, Carol. "The Research Paper as Problem Solving."
In Activating the Passive Student, pp. 144-51.
Research paper unit organized as a series of exercises
that make use of small groups and that encourage students to view each stage in the process as a set of
problems to be solved.

Davis, Beulah. "A Class Paper Approach to the Research
Paper." Teaching English in the Two-Year College, 7

(Spring 1981), 201-03. A paper researched and written by the class as a whole as a prelude to individual projects.

Ford, James E., ed. <u>Teaching the Research Paper: From Theory to Practice, from Research to Writing</u>. New York: Modern Language Association, 1983. Collection of essays on all aspects of the research paper.

Freeman, Alma S. "The Research Paper: Getting Started." In <u>Teaching the Basics--Really!</u> pp. 58-62. Activities that make use of contemporary approaches to teaching composing and that stress the process of discovering materials and writing the research paper.

Grasso, Mary Ellen. "The Research Paper: Life Centered." <u>CE</u>, 40 (September 1978), 83-86. Claims that topics with personal relevance lead to better papers.

Hashimoto, Irvin Y., Barry M. Kroll, and John C. Schafer. <u>Strategies for Academic Writing</u>. Ann Arbor: Univ. of Michigan Press, 1982. Introduction to thinking, planning, researching, and writing a wide range of academic papers; numerous exercises as well as a casebook containing materials for a "controlled sources" paper.

Knodt, Ellen Andrews. "A Path Through the Maze: A Sequential Approach to Writing Documented Papers." In <u>Teaching the Basics--Really!</u> pp. 63-66. Short written assignments give students experience in writing research papers before undertaking a full-scale task.

Marshall, Colleen. "A System for Teaching College Freshmen to Write a Research Paper." <u>CE</u>, 40 (September 1978), 87-90. Uses analytical reading, personal responses to topics, and opinion papers as preparatory steps for the writing of a research paper.

Shamoon, Linda, and Robert A. Schwegler. "Teaching the Research Paper: A New Approach to an Old Problem." <u>FEN</u>, 11 (Spring 1982), 14-17. Argues that current approaches treat the academic research paper as an informative or persuasive essay but that it should be viewed instead as an attempt to shed light on a subject. Provides questions to encourage students to view the research paper in this way.

Taylor, Lee Roger, Jr. "Teaching Freshmen Research Methods." <u>Teaching English in the Two-Year College</u>, 7 (Fall 1980), 37-40. Presents problems that require students to use bibliographic research; solving the problems helps teach research methods and bibliographic form.

Woods, William F. "The Interview as a Practical Research Model." In <u>Activating the Passive Student</u>, pp. 131-38. The interview as a means of research; the "interview paper" as a way to develop skills for later use in research writing.

Practical Writing

Knapp, Joan T. "Teaching Creative Business Letters and
   Memos." In Structuring for Success in the English
   Classroom, pp. 88-91. Suggests having students write
   letters or memos from all the parties involved in a
   sequence of interchanges in some common business
   situation.
Roundy, Nancy. "Heuristics in Student and Professional Composition." The English Record, 33 (Spring 1982), 10-14.
   Strategies for generating and structuring job-related
   writing and ways to teach the strategies in the composition classroom by having students create "cases,"
   i.e., writing situations.

EVALUATION/PEER GRADING

Brannon, Lil, and C. H. Knoblauch. "On Students' Rights to
   Their Own Texts: A Model of Teacher Response." CCC, 33
   (May 1982), 157-66. Argues that to respond more
   effectively to student writing we need to pay more
   attention to the student's intentions and less to our
   preconceived ideas about what the text ought to be.
Christenbury, Leila. "Structuring the Classroom for Peer
   Revision of Composition." In Structuring for Success
   in the English Classroom, pp. 120-25. Activities,
   grouping patterns, and assignment sheets.
Cooper, Charles R., and Lee Odell, eds. Evaluating Writing:
   Describing, Measuring, Judging. Urbana, Ill.: NCTE,
   1977. Essays on a variety of techniques for evaluation,
   including primary trait scoring, holistic grading, and
   evaluating syntactic maturity.
Dietrich, Julia C. "Explaining One's Rhetorical Choices."
   CCC, 29 (May 1978), 195-96. Suggests that giving
   students a chance to submit, along with their papers, a
   paragraph explaining the strategies they chose can help
   reveal the cause of problems and help distinguish
   attempts at growth from real errors.
Ford, James E., and Gregory Larkin. "The Portfolio System:
   An End to Backsliding Writing Standards." CE, 39 (April
   1978), 950-55. A teacher other than the classroom instructor evaluates a portfolio of a student's writing to
   help ensure uniform and fair grading throughout a composition program.
Harris, Muriel. "Evaluation: The Process for Revision."
   JBW, 1 (Spring/Summer 1978), 82-90. Small-group dis-

cussion in the prewriting stage and more formal group
critiques of drafts can help students revise their
work.

Hawkins, Thom. Group Inquiry Techniques for Teaching
Writing. Urbana, Ill.: NCTE, 1976. Theoretical background for small-group instruction and practical advice
for setting up groups and peer criticism.

Hays, Janice. "Facilitating the Peer Critiquing of Writing."
In Structuring for Success in the English Classroom,
pp. 113-19. Practical suggestions for peer criticism:
setting up groups, copying papers, establishing critical
standards.

Jacko, Carol M. "Small-Group Triad: An Instructional Mode
for the Teaching of Writing." CCC, 29 (October 1978),
290-92. Identifies the triad as the most effective size
for small-group instruction in writing; describes roles
that each member must play.

James, David R. "Peer Teaching in the Writing Classroom."
English Journal, 70 (November 1981), 48-50. Reviews
current discussions of peer teaching and evaluation;
bibliography.

Johnston, Brian. "Non-Judgmental Responses to Students'
Writing." English Journal, 71 (April 1982), 50-53.
Nonjudgmental responses can help students assess their
own work and provide stronger motivation than judgmental
responses. Describes different kinds of nonjudgmental
responses.

Knoblauch, C. H., and Lil Brannon. "Teacher Commentary on
Student Writing: The State of the Art." FEN, 10 (Fall
1981), 1-4. Review of research suggests that an emphasis on revision and on the process of writing is more
important than the particular evaluation technique used
to comment on essays.

McDonald, W. U., Jr. "The Revising Process and the Marking
of Student Papers." CCC, 29 (May 1978), 167-70. Argues
that assignments should allow students to submit drafts
for evaluation; believes that comments on early drafts
should deal with broad matters like focus and structure
and only the most serious grammar problems, but that
later comments should be thorough.

Miller, Linda P. "A Conference Methodology for Freshman Composition." Teaching English in the Two-Year College,
7 (Fall 1980), 23-26. Reviews different approaches to
individual conferences and suggests a way of using conferences to intervene in the process of writing and revising.

Olsen, Gary A. "Beyond Evaluation: The Recorded Response to
Essays." Teaching English in the Two-Year College, 8

(Winter 1982), 121-23. Suggests using cassette
recorders to tape evaluations of student papers.
Schiff, Peter. "Responding to Writing: Peer Critiques,
Teacher-Student Conferences, and Essay Evaluations." In
Language Connections: Writing and Reading Across the
Curriculum. Urbana, Ill.: NCTE, 1982, pp. 153-65.
Suggestions for effective peer critiques, descriptions
of different kinds of conferences (e.g., student ques-
tions conference, in-class conference, rewrite confer-
ence), and guidelines for evaluations.
Stanford, Gene, ed. How to Handle the Paper Load. Includes
a number of articles of interest: Neil Ellman, "Struc-
turing Peer Evaluation for Greater Student Indepen-
dence"; David A. England, "Objectives for Our Own Com-
posing Processes—When We Respond to Students"; Mary
Louise Foster and Patricia Markey Naranjo, "Peer
Evaluation: One Approach"; Isabel Hawley, "Critique
Groups for Composition Classes"; Muriel Harris, "The
Overgraded Paper: Another Case of More Is Less"; Sheila
Ann Lisman, "The Best of All Possible Worlds: Where X
Replaces AWK"; Thomas Newkirk, "Read the Papers in
Class"; Audrey J. Roth, "Editorial Groups"; Linda
Shadiow, "Eureka! Moments and Reflection Questions";
R. Baird Shuman, "How to Grade Student Writing" and
"Writing Roulette: Taking a Chance on Not Grading."

SENTENCE COMBINING

Combs, Warren E. "Further Effects of Sentence-Combining
Practice on Writing Ability." Research in the Teaching
of English, 10 (1976), 137-49. Indicates that syntactic
complexity in student papers can be increased by
sentence-combining exercises and that evaluators give
high ratings to papers that display complex syntax.
Cooper, Charles R. "An Outline for Writing Sentence-Combining Problems." English Journal, 62 (January 1973), 96-
102, 108. (Tate and Corbett, pp. 368-78.) Instructions
for writing various kinds of sentence-combining problems, along with numerous examples.
Daiker, Donald, Andrew Kerek, and Max Morenberg. "Sentence-
Combining and Syntactic Maturity in Freshman English."
CCC, 29 (February 1978), 36-41. Presents the results of
an experiment demonstrating the effectiveness of sentence combining over fifteen weeks of intensive
instruction.
Schwegler, Robert A., M. Beverly Swan, and Alison Burns-Katz.
"Sentence Combining and Paragraph Building with
Warriner's." The English Record, 32 (Summer 1981), 18-

21. Describes different kinds of sentence combining:
cued and uncued exercises, retrieving kernels from sentences containing errors, paragraph building, and paragraph rebuilding (comparing student paragraphs to the
original). Shows how to create exercises from materials
in standard textbooks.

Swan, M. Beverly. "Sentence Combining in College Composition: Interim Measures and Patterns." Research in the
Teaching of English, 13 (October 1979), 217-24. Reports
that the amount of instruction students receive in sentence combining is less important than the amount of
time they are given to absorb the instruction. Suggests
that instruction should take place over a relatively
long period, perhaps a fifteen-week semester.

Strong, William. "Sentence Combining: Back to the Basics
and Beyond." English Journal, 65 (February 1976), 56,
60-64. Explains different kinds of exercises and
suggests ways to use them in class.

SETTING UP A WRITING LAB

Beck, Paula, Thom Hawkins, and Marcia Silver. "Training and
Using Peer Tutors." CE, 40 (December 1978), 432-49.
Brief essays on setting up a peer-tutoring program,
training peer tutors, preparing materials and methods,
and evaluating programs.

Harris, Muriel, ed. Tutoring Writing: A Sourcebook for
Writing Labs. Glenview, Ill.: Scott, Foresman, 1982.
A collection of essays on all aspects of setting up and
running a writing lab, including diagnosing writing
problems and training tutors. Includes sample forms for
referring students and recording progress.

Hawkins, Thom, and Phyllis Brooks, eds. New Directions for
College Learning Assistance: Improving Writing Skills.
San Francisco: Jossey-Bass, 1981. Essays on designing
labs, varieties of tutoring strategies, training tutors,
administrative arrangements, evaluation, and the relationship of research to the writing lab.

Podis, Leonard A. "Training Peer Tutors for the Writing
Lab." CCC, 31 (February 1980), 70-75. Describes in
detail a course for training peer tutors.

Steward, Joyce S., and Mary K. Croft. The Writing Lab-
oratory: Organization, Management, and Methods.
Glenview, Ill.: Scott, Foresman, 1982. Practical advice
for running a lab: financing; physical arrangements;
selecting, training, and supervising staff; kinds of
instruction; scheduling, reporting, and evaluating.

Provides sample forms, promotional materials, and sample lesson outlines.

Waldrep, Thomas E., ed. "Writing Centers: Redefining, Reassessing, Reaffirming." A special issue of The CEA Forum, 12 (February 1982). Articles on the operation and staffing of writing labs, with suggested readings.

Answers to Exercises

Part I

THE WHOLE PAPER AND PARAGRAPHS

Chapter 1 Developing an Essay

EXERCISE 1, p. 7. No sample answers.

EXERCISE 2, p. 7. No sample answers.

EXERCISE 3, p. 7

Sample answers:

1. The interior of a 1930s diner
2. The typical villain in old gangster movies
3. A windy winter day at the lake
4. The appearance of a homely wooden chair
5. The differences between Time and Newsweek
6. The influences of the Rolling Stones on rock music
7. What is a sports car?
8. How to look at a painting
9. Spending a lonely Saturday night on campus
10. My first college swimming meet
11. A day in the life of a full-time student and a full-time worker
12. The plot of a typical spy thriller
13. Why students should have to study a foreign language
14. Why the federal government should support cultural programming on TV
15. Why the drinking age should be lowered to eighteen throughout the nation
16. Why the U.S. president should be limited to a single six-year term

EXERCISE 4, p. 12. No sample answers.

EXERCISE 5, p. 12.   No sample answers.

EXERCISE 6, p. 13.   No sample answers.

EXERCISE 7, p. 14.   No sample answers.

EXERCISE 8, p. 18

1. Both halves of the sentence need to be more specific:
    What kind of gun control? Essential for what end?
    Possible revision: To curb the rising rate of murder with
    handguns, restrictions on the sale of handguns should be
    legislated and strictly enforced.
    The sentence implies a persuasive purpose, an argumenta-
    tive essay.
2. Good thesis sentence: limited, specific, and unified. It
    implies an informative purpose, a narrative essay.
3. Both good manners and make our society work need to be
    more specific.
    Possible revision: Courtesy between people makes human
    interaction smoother and more efficient.
    The sentence implies an informative and perhaps also per-
    suasive purpose, an expository essay.
4. Different needs limiting.
    Possible revision: City people are different from
    country people in their attitudes toward strangers, poli-
    ticians, and money.
    The sentence implies an informative purpose, an exposi-
    tory essay.
5. The sentence lacks unity because the first half is posi-
    tive but not very specific, while the second half is
    negative and specific. To unify the sentence, make the
    first half more specific and the second half positive.
    Possible revision: Television is both a useful baby
    sitter for children, offering them education and enter-
    tainment, and a good escape for adults, providing them
    with relief from their own problems.
    The sentence implies an informative purpose, an exposi-
    tory essay.
6. The word best is vague; it needs to be made more specific
    to give perspective to the essay.
    Possible revision: The most entertaining rock concerts
    are those in which the performers transform a passive
    crowd into a stamping, screaming mob.

The sentence implies a purpose of informing or entertaining in an expository, narrative, or descriptive essay.

7. The sentence is a flat statement of personal preference that provides no preview of reasons for the preference. Possible revision: Although I liked American history in high school, when the teacher focused on social trends and events, I do not like it in college because the teacher focuses on political events and personalities. The sentence implies an informative purpose, an expository essay.

8. The sentence lacks unity because the two halves do not clearly relate to each other. Possible revision: We should not be encouraged to choose a career in college because a person should delay a career decision until he or she has worked in several jobs. The sentence implies a persuasive purpose, an argumentative essay.

9. The sentence lacks unity because the clause whose . . . impaired is not directly related to the opinion being stated. Possible revision: Drivers who have demonstrated bad judgment and lack of control by operating a car under the influence of alcohol should receive mandatory suspensions of their licenses. The sentence implies a persuasive purpose, an argumentative essay.

10. The sentence is not specific enough about the qualities that make the beach not lonely. Possible revision: The beach in winter, far from being a lonely place, is a source of comforting sights and sounds. The sentence implies an informative and perhaps self-expressive purpose, a descriptive essay.

EXERCISE 9, p. 19.   No sample answers.

EXERCISE 10, p. 19

Sample answers:

1. Blue jeans etiquette demands the old worn pair on some occasions and the new tight pair on others.

2. Helping my friend overcome drug dependency taught me how to be patient and consistent in my dealings with others.
3. Traveling reveals aspects of human nature that are not apparent under less stressful circumstances.
4. Everyone should live for a while in an old building, for old walls and floors provide an essential sense of continuity with the past.
5. The sounds of the city at midnight conjure up a dual image of people having fun and people in trouble.
6. As long as they do not have children, married people should be able to divorce easily so that they can seek happier, more stable relationships elsewhere.
7. To care for a plant, one must understand and fulfill its special needs for sunlight, water, and nutrition.
8. Most students seem to attend college for one of three reasons: to prepare for a career, to enhance social life, or to delay the decisions of adulthood.
9. Deciding whom to vote for in an election requires looking beneath the superficial qualities of candidates to the principles that guide their words and actions.
10. As long as women are considered too precious or too fragile for combat, they will never be fully equal to men.
11. Tracing the rumor of Mr. Petrieka's secret sin revealed a laughable series of misunderstood conversations.
12. My vision of the ideal car is surely not too demanding: trunk space for more than two suitcases, a back seat large enough for two grown people, reasonable gas mileage, and the spunk to enter the freeway safely.
13. An expanded transportation system is essential to reduce congestion, noise, and choking smog in the city.
14. For the two months I stayed with my ex-roommate, his slothfulness, rudeness, and deceit caused me constant pain.
15. A golf tournament like this year's U.S. Open demonstrates the game's often-overlooked potential for excitement.

EXERCISE 11, p. 23

Sample answers:

1. For elementary school students: physical effects in simple terms; statistics in simple figures; difficulty of quitting once addicted; importance of resisting peer pressure. For adult smokers: graphic depiction of physical effects; detailed statistics; influence on children; effect on smoker's appearance, odor, breath.

2. For someone who is on welfare: help for children; possi-
    bility that government support will lead to self-support;
    need for bureaucracy to manage system; need for periodic
    checks to protect against cheating by a few recipients.
    For someone who opposes welfare: need to provide for
    people who can't work; need to provide for children; low
    cost relative to other budget expenditures; low incidence
    of cheating.
3. For the camper: chance to get out of the dirty city;
    opportunity to swim and hike; chance to meet other chil-
    dren; chance to get away from parents.
    For the parents: low cost; expert staff; constructive
    experience; opportunity to be free of the child.
4. For your neighbors: angry feelings of neighborhood resi-
    dents; dangers to children and pets; lowered property
    values; threat of petition to zoning board.
    For the zoning board: violation of zoning regulations;
    length of time wrecked truck has been present; number of
    unsuccessful appeals to neighbors; dangers to children
    and pets.
5. For someone who has never experienced snow: the air during
    snowfall; how snow accumulates on ground; appearance after
    snowfall of trees, buildings, and so on; muffled sounds
    after snowfall.
    For someone who hates snow: interruption of boring rou-
    tine caused by heavy snow; cheering effect of snowfall
    on children; peace and quiet of city during and after
    snowfall; snow's protection of plants against cold.

EXERCISE 12, p. 24

1. Toward the subject: disparaging, derisive, yet indulgent.
    Toward readers: expectation of agreement, shared humor.
2. Toward the subject: sympathetic, frustrated.
    Toward readers: inviting same view of subject, shared
    powerlessness.
3. Toward the subject: obvious enjoyment in details of sense
    experience.
    Toward readers: folksy, chatty, inviting.

EXERCISE 13, p. 25. No sample answers.

EXERCISE 14, p. 34

Sample answers:

1. Bizarre hairdo; strangely made-up face; old, ragged,
   baggy clothes; impeccable white tennis shoes.
2. One student swims laps. Another goes to movies. Another
   drinks beer. They all try to divert attention away from
   whatever caused the frustration or tension.
3. To study for an examination: clear your mind and work
   space; review class notes; review the text; organize the
   material in your own way.
4. Eighteen-year-olds, as a group, are not mature enough to
   handle the responsibilities and effects of drinking.
   They should not be legally tempted into alcoholism. Still
   concerned with creating an impression of competence, they
   would not refuse to drive when drunk. They cannot assimi-
   late the extreme emotions of drunkenness into their normal behavior.
5. First, an objective view of those left behind; second, a
   gradual fading of the earthly world; third, an expanding
   bright light from above; fourth, a brilliant, peaceful,
   eternal presence.
6. In baby-sitting: the obvious activities of obtaining
   emergency numbers, tending to the children's needs, keeping the house clean; the less obvious activity of giving
   the children some worthwhile lesson while reading, story
   telling, or playing.
7. Sarah and Nancy are both intelligent, both sensitive.
   But Sarah is sensitive to the feelings of others, whereas
   Nancy is sensitive primarily to her own feelings.
8. To satisfy my parents; to make new friends; to play baseball; but mostly to learn something about the world before
   entering it.
9. They can provide methods of achieving goals. They can
   provide insights into the behavior of oneself and others.
   In general, they can help people with problems feel as if
   they have support in solving those problems.
10. It increases one's physical and mental health. It is
    good for the heart and muscles. It keeps weight down.
    It makes one feel good about oneself.

EXERCISE 15, p. 34

Possible revision (changes underlined):

   I. Reasons for strip-mining
       A. Need for coal because of energy shortage
       B. Advantages over underground mining
           1. Quicker
           2. Less expensive
           3. Safer
  II. Effects of strip-mining
       A. Pollution of water resources
           1. Causes
               a. Leaching of soil acids by rainwater
               b. Run-off of acids into streams
           2. Results
               a. Disappearance of fish
               b. Poisoning of water supply
       B. Destruction of the land
           1. Appearance
               a. Scarring
               b. Destruction of vegetation
           2. Erosion
               a. Removal of topsoil
               b. Danger of mud slides
           3. Elimination of people's forms of recreation
               a. Fishing
               b. Camping and hiking
       C. Devastation of people's lives
           1. Illness from water pollution
           2. Destruction of farmland and homes
               a. Acid soil
               b. Mud slides
               c. Inadequate compensation
 III. Possible controls on strip-mining
       A. Regulation of mining techniques
           1. Limitations on erosion
           2. Limitations on pollution
       B. Mandatory reclamation of land
           1. Replacement of topsoil
           2. Restoration of vegetation
       C. Required compensation for farmers and home
           owners
           1. Cash payments
           2. Rebuilding

EXERCISE 16, p. 35

The following points do not support the thesis:

> Food: whom to tip
> Car: unlimited gas, danger of theft, expensive upkeep
> Travel: learn to see the benefits of the U.S., health
>   hazards
> Problems: Though these points might provide an ironic
>   conclusion to the essay, none belongs in the body
>   of the paper because none supports the thesis

EXERCISE 17, p. 36

List of details:

> at dinner parties, elbow, seating arrangements
> as a child, told to use right hand
> few left-handed desk chairs
> can't make scissors work properly
> upside-down writing
> leprosy or social disease

General statements:

> being left-handed has no benefits
> it's a condition with no pluses, unless you like being
>   disadvantaged

To rearrange the paragraph, begin with a generalization that
contains the topic:

> Being left-handed has no benefits.

Then arrange details in chronological order:

> As a child, you are constantly told to use your right
> hand. You can't even make scissors work properly. In
> school there are few left-handed desk chairs. And when
> you write, you look to others as if you're writing
> upside-down.
>
> At dinner parties, you have to eat with your elbow tucked
> into your ribs, or you have to make a fuss about the
> seating arrangements.

Conclude with the last generalization and with the analogy that expands the word condition:

> It's a condition with no pluses, unless you like being disadvantaged. It's as if you have leprosy or a social disease.

EXERCISE 18, p. 36.   No sample answers.

Chapter 2   Writing and Revising the Essay

EXERCISE 1, p. 41

The questions in this exercise are answered in Balik's own revisions and in the text discussion of them, pages 44-47 of the handbook.

EXERCISE 2, p. 52.   No sample answers.

EXERCISE 3, p. 53.   No sample answers.

EXERCISE 4, p. 53

The numbers below match the question numbers in the exercise instruction. (Note that both essays are further analyzed in the answer to Chapter 3, Exercise 19.)

"The Gentle Manatee," p. 53

1. The first paragraph indicates that the writer's purpose is both informing and persuading, but the body of the paper is entirely expository.
2. The thesis sentence is really two sentences (the last two in the first paragraph), and together they do not clearly preview the writer's topic or purpose. The first of the two sentences employs vague terms: a virtue, add variety to the world. The somewhat persuasive stance of this sentence is lost in the second sentence, whose informative purpose in fact seems to guide the development of the essay.

3. The writer covers the manatee's habitat, food, and population (paragraph 2), breeding and size (3), appearance
(4), and behavior (5 and 6)--thus, apparently, moving
from subsistence patterns to more outward social behavior.
But the writer seems uncertain of how to handle the details, and the scheme is not wholly consistent. Paragraph 2 (first sentence) refers to the manatee as huge,
but not until paragraph 3 does the reader learn how huge.
The reduction in population from motorboats (paragraph 2)
and the slow breeding cycle (paragraph 3) should be connected in one paragraph on population. The manatee's
harmlessness (paragraph 5) would more logically come
after the animal's ideal existence (paragraph 6), since
harmlessness is called the "most interesting characteristic" and is echoed in the conclusion.

4. The essay's strongest feature is its wealth of specific
information about manatees. Every idea in the body of
the essay is well supported with facts and descriptive
details.

5. The writer's serious, thoughtful tone reveals his own
deep respect and concern for manatees. His intended
audience seems to be people who do not know about manatees and who might also be moved to concern for them.

"Working in the Barnyard," p. 54

1. The writer's purpose seems to be both self-expressive and
informative. The essay is narrative.

2. The thesis sentence (the last sentence of paragraph 1)
clearly and specifically states the writer's topic (a
work experience) and perspective on that topic (learning
something valuable).

3. The essay's pattern of organization is clearly chronological. The writer adheres to the organization throughout, providing ample time signals to help the reader
follow the narrative (for example, Last May, then, as
soon as I arrived).

4. This otherwise very competent essay is marred by omis-
sions of concrete details and examples that would give
the reader a sense of actually sharing the experience
instead of rushing through it. Paragraph 2: What did
Mrs. King look like? How huge were the mail shipments?
Paragraph 3: What were some of the actual words spoken
by the writer and Mrs. King? Paragraph 4: What was in-
efficient about delivery routes and times for coffee
breaks? What exactly did Mrs. King do or say in reacting
to the writer's questions? Paragraph 5: In what specific

ways did the writer pester Mrs. King? How were the
efforts fruitless? How counterproductive? What snide
names did Mrs. King use? How did she pick on the writer's
work? What reprimands did she issue?
5. The writer's tone is straightforward yet subdued--
strangely subdued when she tells of Mrs. King's tyranny.
We sense from the beginning that the writer was humbled
by this experience, and the last paragraph is genuinely
humble in tone. The writer seems to conceive of her
readers as other inexperienced workers like herself, and
her attitude toward them is confiding.

Chapter 3   Composing Good Paragraphs

EXERCISE 1, p. 66

1. The central idea is in sentence 1. The shape is △ .
2. The central idea is in sentences 1 and 4. The shape is
   � .
3. The central idea is in sentence 2. The shape is ✕ .
4. The central idea is in sentence 1, and it is further
   limited in sentences 2 and 6. The shape is △ .

EXERCISE 2, p. 65

1. The topic sentence is sentence 1. Unrelated are sentences 4 and 7.
2. The topic sentence is sentence 1, clarified in sentence
   2. Unrelated are sentences 5, 6, and 7.

EXERCISE 3, p. 66

Delete statements not pertaining to Mozart's accomplishments:
when he was born, where he lived, when he married, his debts.
Possible paragraph:

Mozart's accomplishments in music seem remarkable
even today. At the age of six he made his first concert
tour of Europe, playing harpsichord, organ, and violin.
He had begun composing music at the age of five, and by
adolescence he had published numerous musical compositions. When he died at thirty-five, his work included

over six hundred compositions, most notably operas, symphonies, quartets, and piano concertos.

EXERCISE 4, p. 66.   No sample answers.

EXERCISE 5, p. 78

1. The paragraph topic is stated in sentence 1 and is restricted in sentences 2 and 3. The paragraph is organized from general to specific.
2. The paragraph topic is stated in sentence 1. The details are arranged chronologically.
3. The paragraph topic is stated in sentence 6. The details are arranged spatially.
4. The paragraph topic is stated in sentence 1 and is restricted in sentence 2. The details are arranged from general to specific.

EXERCISE 6, p. 79

1. The central idea is in sentence 3. A coherent order would be 1, 3, 2, 6, 4, 7, 5.
2. The central idea is in sentence 2. A coherent order would be 2, 1, 5, 7, 6, 4, 3, 8.

EXERCISE 7, p. 80

1. Parallelism and repetition in sentences 2, 3, and 4: They have measured; They have recorded and studied; they have learned. Repetition of whale, sings, and song throughout. Pronoun they substituting for scientists throughout. And (sentence 4) serves as transitional expression.
2. Repetition of world in sentences 1, 2, and 3; ingredient(s) in 5 and 6; Coca-Cola and Coke in 1, 3, 4, and 5. Transitional words: Moreover (3), Yet (4), And (6). Pronouns: It or its for Coca-Cola in 2 and 4.
3. Parallelism and repetition of Your parents must be so proud (1) and my parents were proud (2). Repetition of proud and pride in sentences 1, 2, and 4; parents and parental in 1, 2, and 4; education in 1, 2, and 3. Pronouns: they for parents in 2 and 3. Transitional expressions: too (2), also (4).

4. Parallelism in description of pocket contents (sentences
   8 and 10) and within many sentences. Repetition and restatement abound: <u>mouth</u> and <u>lips</u>, 1, 2, 3, and 6; <u>pucker</u>
   and <u>puckered</u>, 3 and 4; <u>pucker</u>, <u>smile</u>, and <u>both expres-</u>
   <u>sions</u>, 3, 4, and 5; <u>pocket</u> or <u>pockets</u>, 1, 6, 7, 9, and
   10. Pronouns: <u>he</u> or <u>his</u>, 1, 2, 3, 6, 7, 10, and 11;
   <u>They</u>, 8. Transitional expressions: <u>After</u>, 4; <u>In addition</u>,
   9; <u>When</u>, 11.

EXERCISE 8, p. 80

Inconsistency in number: <u>males</u> and <u>provider</u>, sentence 1. Inconsistency in verb tense: <u>needed</u> and <u>work</u>, sentence 2; <u>did</u>
and <u>is</u>, sentence 3; <u>enjoy</u> and <u>have been</u>, sentence 4. Inconsistency in person: <u>one</u> and <u>your</u>, sentence 3. Possible revision:

> I rebel against the idea of <u>the male</u> always being
> the sole family provider. For me to be happy, I <u>need</u> to
> feel useful, and so I work to support myself and <u>my</u>
> daughter. I <u>do</u> not feel that it is wrong for one (or <u>a</u>
> <u>woman</u>) to be a housewife while a man supports <u>one</u> (or
> <u>her</u>), but that way is not for me. I enjoy the business
> world, and I <u>am</u> pleased with my job. Working, I make
> enough now to support the two of us, and I know that
> when I graduate, I will be able to earn even more. I
> can do very well as my own provider.

EXERCISE 9, p. 80

Possible paragraph (the two restrictions of the topic sentence
are underlined):

> The advantages of hypnosis over drugs have not been
> fully recognized or exploited. <u>Hypnosis is far superior</u>
> <u>to drugs for relieving tension.</u> It is not nearly as ex-
> pensive as drugs, even for people who have not learned
> self-hypnosis. It has none of the dangerous side effects
> of drugs. And, perhaps most important, hypnosis is non-
> addicting. <u>Moreover, hypnosis can do things drugs can-</u>
> <u>not do.</u> It can help people sleep soundly, awake re-
> freshed, and stay alert and productive. It can help
> people overcome self-destructive habits like smoking and
> overeating. And it can permanently boost self-confidence
> and morale.

EXERCISE 10, p. 81.   No sample answers.

EXERCISE 11, p. 90

1. Sentences 2, 3, and 4 should each be followed by at least two specific examples of gestures to make the writer's meaning concrete.
2. Specific facts are needed to support the broad assertions of sentences 2 and 3: What are the expenses of married working students compared to those of single people?
3. Sentences 2 and 3 require specific support, perhaps both citations of studies that have demonstrated the effects mentioned and examples of children's behavior.

EXERCISE 12, p. 91.   No sample answers.

EXERCISE 13, p. 91

1. The paragraph is developed by a combination of illustration (examples of computers' speed) and comparison and contrast (computer time and human time). Specific details appear in sentences 2, 3, and 4.
2. The paragraph is developed by division of a dying person's attitude into five stages. Specific details appear in sentences 2–6, each sentence a description of a separate stage.
3. The paragraph is developed by a combination of comparison and contrast (the activities of old and young people) and cause-and-effect analysis (the effects of stifling limitations on old people's activities). Specific details appear in sentences 4, 5, 8, 9, and 11.
4. The paragraph is developed by a definition of mooches. Specific details appear particularly in sentences 3 and 5.
5. The paragraph is developed by a combination of cause-and-effect analysis (the causes of the plague) and comparison and contrast (the actual causes of the plague and the imagined causes in the fourteenth century). Specific details appear in sentences 2, 3, 5, and 7.

EXERCISE 14, p. 93

Possible answers:

1. cause-and-effect analysis
2. illustration
3. process analysis
4. comparison and contrast
5. support with reasons
6. definition
7. classification
8. illustration or definition
9. analogy
10. cause-and-effect analysis

EXERCISE 15, p. 93.   No sample answers.

EXERCISE 16, p. 93.   No sample answers.

EXERCISE 17, p. 99

The introductory and concluding paragraphs in the first draft (pp. 38 and 40) are both too abrupt. The introductory paragraph, consisting only of the thesis sentence, fails to ease the reader from the outside world into the essay and thus fails to generate curiosity about either the topic or the writer's approach to it. The concluding paragraph suddenly introduces an apparently new idea (games are meant to be played between people) and fails to tie off several strands of the essay, such as the relative advantages of computer games. In contrast, the final-draft paragraphs (pp. 49 and 51) are considerably improved. The introductory paragraph pulls the reader into the writer's world by starting with the familiar idea of computer games' popularity and gradually leading to the thesis sentence. The concluding paragraph clarifies the source of the idea in the first draft and shows how the idea relates to the rest of the essay.

EXERCISE 18, p. 99.   No sample answers.

EXERCISE 19, p. 102

1. Essay on p. 49: Each paragraph in the body of the essay
    relates directly to a quality named in the thesis sen-
    tence: computer games' speed of play (paragraph 2), ex-
    citement (3), and challenge (4); Monopoly's staying power
    (5) and opportunity for interaction (6). Paragraph 2
    begins with a transition from the opening paragraph, and
    paragraph 5 begins with a transition from the preceding
    paragraphs that signals a shift in focus. Paragraphs 3,
    4, and 6 each begin with a statement of the paragraph's
    topic, and the openings of 4 and 6 further remind readers
    of where they are in the comparison. Transitional markers
    appear in all paragraphs: for instance, in contrast (3),
    one other distinct advantage (4), So far (5), An even
    greater advantage (6). (Further analysis of this essay
    appears in Chapter 2 of the handbook.)

2. Essay on p. 53: The essay's thesis is unspecific, so the
    relations between it and the body paragraphs are difficult
    to see; no paragraph except the conclusion echoes the
    thesis. Only the third and fourth paragraphs are ex-
    plicitly linked; otherwise, the paragraphs seem simply to
    be tacked on, one after the other. The opening sentences
    of the fourth and fifth paragraphs even contradict each
    other: appearance is called the most remarkable thing
    about a manatee, and harmlessness is called the most in-
    teresting characteristic. (Further analysis of this
    essay appears in the answer to Chapter 2, Exercise 4.)

3. Essay on p. 54: The paragraphs in this narrative essay
    relate clearly to the thesis and proceed smoothly from
    one incident to the next. Transitions are provided pri-
    marily by time markers such as Last May (second para-
    graph), as soon as I arrived (third paragraph), after
    about a week (fourth paragraph), over the next seven
    weeks (fifth paragraph), Two months after I had started
    work (sixth paragraph), a month before school began (con-
    cluding paragraph). (Further analysis of this essay
    appears in the answer to Chapter 2, Exercise 4.)

EXERCISE 20, p. 102.

1. The central idea in sentence 1 is further limited in
    sentence 2; the shape is △ . The organization is
    general to specific. Coherence is achieved primarily by

repetition and restatement (<u>leisurely</u> . . . <u>contemplation</u>
. . . <u>relaxed, unhurried</u> . . . "<u>pastime</u>"; <u>pastoral</u> . . .
<u>tableau</u> . . . <u>lush green background</u> . . . <u>rural</u> . . . <u>un-</u>
<u>troubled island</u>); by the pronouns <u>it</u> and <u>its</u>; and by the
parallelism of sentences 3 and 4 (<u>In its relaxed, un-</u>
<u>hurried way, it is</u> . . . <u>Born in a rural age, it offers</u>
<u>. . .</u>). The paragraph is developed by illustration and
to some extent by explicit and implicit comparison with
other games.

2. The central idea is in sentence 4; the shape is ⧖ .
The organization is roughly chronological. Coherence is
achieved by transitional expressions (<u>During, Yet, When</u>);
by the pronouns <u>she</u> and <u>her</u>; and by the parallel subject-
verb patterns in most of the sentences (<u>My grandmother</u>
<u>was one</u> . . . <u>She was</u> . . . <u>she lived</u>, and so on). The
paragraph is developed by illustration.

3. The central idea in sentence 1 is clarified in sentences
2 and 3; the shape is △ . The organization is general
to specific. Coherence is achieved primarily by repetition and restatement (<u>White House</u> . . . <u>White House</u>;
<u>barnyard</u> . . . <u>chickens</u> . . . <u>chicken</u> . . . <u>barnyard</u>;
<u>pecking order</u> . . . <u>peck</u> . . . <u>pecked</u> . . . <u>pecking order</u>)
and by transitional expressions (<u>only, The first, The</u>
<u>second</u>). The paragraph is developed by analogy.

4. The term <u>transistor</u> is introduced in sentence 1, but the
paragraph's central idea--a definition of the transistor--
is not stated in a single sentence. The organization is
general to specific, in that the attributes of transistors
become increasingly specific, and also somewhat climactic,
in that the important attributes of size and cheapness
are saved for last. Coherence is achieved by the pro-
nouns <u>they</u> and <u>their</u>; by repetition and restatement (<u>hard-</u>
<u>ware</u> . . . <u>transistor</u> . . . <u>transistors</u> . . . <u>devices</u>
<u>. . . devices</u> . . . <u>transistors</u>); by the transitional
expression <u>Moreover</u>; and by parallelism (<u>They are solid</u>
<u>. . . they are stones</u> . . . <u>They are durable</u>). The para-
graph is developed by definition.

5. The central idea is in sentence 2; the shape is △ . The
organization is chronological. Coherence is achieved by
transitional expressions (<u>First, Second, Finally</u>); by the
pronoun <u>they</u>; and by parallelism (<u>they should shop around</u>
<u>. . . they should consult guides</u> . . . <u>they should refuse</u>
<u>to accept</u> . . . <u>demand to see</u> . . . <u>decline to sign or</u>
<u>accept</u>). The paragraph is developed by process analysis.

6. The central idea is in sentence 1; the shape is △ .
The organization is general to specific. Coherence is
achieved primarily by repetition and restatement (for

instance, <u>small versus large animals . . . small animals
. . . large animals . . . large mammals . . . small animals . . . tiny shrews . . . blue whales; life . . .
life . . . life . . . lives</u>). The paragraph is developed
by comparison and contrast.
7. The central idea is in sentences 1 and 8; the shape is
    ◇ . The organization is specific to general. Coherence
    is achieved by some parallelism (<u>Looking at a loved child
    . . . seeing a child</u>); by transitional expressions
    (<u>This</u>, <u>Nor</u>, <u>For</u>); and especially by repetition and re-
    statement (<u>grandparent and grandchild . . . child . . .
    child . . . grandchild . . . grandparent . . . children
    . . . grandfather's . . . grandson's</u>). The paragraph is
    developed primarily by cause-and-effect analysis: the
    effects of the grandparent-grandchild relationship.

Chapter 4   <u>Convincing a Reader</u>

EXERCISE 1, p. 107

Possible revision:

> Drugs and alcohol only seem like ways to escape
from reality. Surely death--one real danger of using
both--is an undesirable escape. All drugs and alcohol
can do is give a minute of relief from disappointment
and frustration. Those who delude themselves into
thinking they are getting anything more are seriously,
and sadly, sick.

EXERCISE 2, p. 107

Possible revisions:

1. Though some knowledge of science is probably essential
    for a well-rounded person, the college's science require-
    ment seems designed to waste students' time.
2. Though some believe the best way to solve the energy
    shortage is to perfect our use of solar energy, we will
    be most successful in the long run if we increase the
    number of nuclear power plants.
3. In a society as advanced as ours, it may seem that mail
    service should be free; however, to be fair to all,
    users should bear the cost of the service.

4. The federal and local governments should certainly moni-
   tor what goes out over the public airways; but, ulti-
   mately, responsibility for children's viewing habits
   rests squarely on the parents.
5. Jailing all convicted criminals for a definite time might
   erase some inequity in our judicial system; but such uniform treatment of law breakers would also eliminate the
   opportunity for merciful application of the law.

EXERCISE 3, p. 112

1. The first and last two sentences are assertions of prejudice. The second sentence is a vague assertion of fact.
2. The first sentence is opinion based on self-knowledge.
   Then follow statements of personal preference.

EXERCISE 4, p. 112

The meaning of current problems is vague and shifting. At
first, the writer seems to mean the high cost of living caused
by scarcities. But in the last sentence a new problem appears:
insecurity. Self-sufficiency is similarly vague, defined only
by the examples of freeing ourselves from grocery and department stores. A possible revision:

> The best solution to one current problem--helpless-
> ness in the face of rising prices--is one you don't hear
> very often: self-sufficiency. If we were more self-
> sufficient, we would not have to rely so much on scarce
> resources to satisfy basic needs. Instead, we could draw
> on our innate or easily learned capacities to provide for
> ourselves. With an inexpensive sewing machine, some
> fabric, some skill, and time, a person can be at least
> partly independent of clothing stores. With a good-
> sized garden, some tools and supplies, and work, a family
> can grow a year's supply of vegetables and be completely
> independent of the grocery store's produce section. Any
> degree of self-sufficiency provides not only the economic
> reward of avoiding high prices, but also the psychologi-
> cal reward of no longer feeling helpless.

EXERCISE 5, p. 112

1. The question is whether many women are bored with their lives. This statement begs the question by assuming the unproved truths that they are bored and that their boredom is caused by tedious jobs.
2. The question is whether Steven McRae is an effective spokesman. The statement ignores the question by presenting an irrelevant observation about his attitude toward himself, an argument ad hominem.
3. The question is whether teenagers should be allowed to drink. This statement begs the question by asserting that teenagers should not be allowed to drink because they are teenagers.
4. The question is what dangers there might be in giving nuclear capability to emerging nations, obviously a complex issue. The statement ignores the complexity of the question by appealing to fear.
5. The question is whether our souls are immortal. The statement begs the question by asserting immortality of the soul as being proved by the soul's immortality.

EXERCISE 6, p. 113.   No sample answers.

EXERCISE 7, p. 115

1. The question to be proved is that a college education does cost much. Details of typical tuition costs, dormitory and meal charges, and book expenses would be appropriate.
2. The assertion is based on what life really is. If M*A*S*H fills in the blank, "life as it really is" could be narrowed to "a doctor's life is not all glamour." Support: There is blood in the operating room; some patients die; even success is exhausting.
3. The development must first establish the characteristics that define good. Then examples of behavior that exhibits those qualities would support the assertion.
4. The question is whether Americans waste energy. Perhaps compare the number of cars (on campus, for example, or in a shopping center parking lot) to the number of bicycles or pedestrians. Mention lights that burn for twenty-four hours and other examples of apparent waste.
5. The question is what makes a great hero and whether Superman has those qualities. If a hero is able to do things

an ordinary human cannot do, Superman is a hero because
he can leap tall buildings. If a hero is modest, Superman is a hero because he hides his identity.

EXERCISE 8, p. 115

1. First, the evidence is inadequate and unrepresentative:
   only one example of our rivers and streams, and only a
   few details of its pollution. Second, the prohibition
   of swimming is not explained; the river's current, hidden
   rocks, or water snakes could be at fault as well. Third,
   the minister is an irrelevant authority.
2. This paragraph does give evidence--examples--of crime,
   though the examples are not representative enough to
   establish that crime is out of control. Some hard facts
   are needed, such as statistics of crime in the last
   month. The three examples can then become illustrations
   to make the facts immediate.

EXERCISE 9, p. 122

The unreasonable generalizations from the given evidence are
statements 1 (contradicted by the facts) and 3 (the reasons
for the population shift are not given in the facts).

EXERCISE 10, p. 122

1. b. Lung cancer can cause death.
2. c. Therefore, biology is a good course.
3. a. Children who receive no individual attention learn
      slowly.
4. b. Warren is a discus thrower.
5. a. The school will close if enrollments decline.

EXERCISE 11, p. 122

Possible revisions:

1. If it could be determined that capital punishment pre-
   vents murder, then death should be the mandatory sentence
   for all murderers.
2. The mayor was previously the president of a manufacturing
   company that ignores controls on air pollution and did so

under his direction as well; therefore, he might not en-
force the controls, and our city may experience increased
air pollution.

3. If it is true that Americans measure success by income,
then the only way to be successful in the United States
is to make money.

4. Keeping the library open until midnight may have con-
tributed to the increase in late-night crime on campus
because more students outside at night means more potential victims of crime.

5. We should all maintain an active interest in government
to ensure the honesty of public officials.

EXERCISE 12, p. 123

1. Hasty generalization. No one is absolute, and age of
twenty-five suggests stereotyping.
A revision: A successful marriage demands a degree of
maturity.

2. Hasty generalization.
A revision: Students' persistent complaints about the
unfairness of the grading system should be investigated.

3. Oversimplification.
A revision: The United States got involved in World
War II for many complex reasons. The bombing of Pearl
Harbor was a triggering incident.

4. Either . . . or fallacy.
A revision: People watch television for many reasons,
but some watch because they are too lazy to talk or read
or because they want mindless escape from their lives.

5. False analogy.
A revision: Some working people see themselves as slaves
to their corporate masters.

6. Hasty generalization.
A revision: Stories about welfare chiselers show that
some people on welfare do shirk and cheat.

7. Post hoc fallacy.
A revision: We wonder whether my cousin's recent three
fainting spells have anything to do with his climbing
Pike's Peak.

8. Oversimplification.
A revision: Racial tension may occur when people with
different backgrounds live side by side.

9. Either . . . or fallacy.
A revision: Failing to supply military assistance to
Central and South American countries may encourage the
spread of Communism.

10. Non sequitur.
     A revision: She admits to being an atheist, so how can
     she be a good Sunday school teacher?

EXERCISE 13, p. 123

This essay is most immoderate in tone. The writer's purpose
might be seen as entertainment, but not persuasion. Exaggeration is common: <u>truly disadvantaged students</u>; <u>never</u>; <u>most mad-
dening</u>. Instead of offering evidence--facts about numbers of
cars and numbers of parking spaces--the writer begs or ignores
the crucial questions of the argument or commits faults in
reasoning. Examples:

     Commuters are regularly treated as second-class citizens.
     [Begs the question. Evidence?]

     If parking were easier, students would get better grades,
     and the school administrators would have the higher en-
     rollments they're so desperate for. [Two non sequiturs.]

     The money probably goes toward a new faculty office
     building or dormitory. [Oversimplification. Evidence?]

     Why should the rich folks in charge of things care what
     happens to a few struggling students . . . ? [<u>Ad hominem</u>
     argument and appeal to pity.]

     The commuting students are like Jews wandering in the
     wilderness. . . . [False analogy.]

Part II

GRAMMATICAL SENTENCES

Chapter 5 Understanding Sentence Grammar

EXERCISE 1, p. 131

```
        Subject|Predicate
1.  The radio fell.
    Sample imitation:  The door opened.
```

```
    Subject|Predicate
2.  Summer ends soon.
    Sample imitation:  Winter lasts forever.
```

```
            Subject|Predicate
3.  My brother's dog had fourteen puppies.
    Sample imitation:  The old refrigerator holds little food.
```

```
    Subject|Predicate
4.  People should think carefully before joining cults.
    Sample imitation:  Teachers may groan loudly while grading
        tests.
```

```
                Subject|Predicate
5.  Several important people will speak at commencement.
    Sample imitation:  Nine small children will appear in the
        play.
```

EXERCISE 2, p. 131

```
         N    P     V      V       N
1.  The trees they planted are dying of blight.
                    N      V             N
2.  The new speed limit has prevented many accidents.
         P  V              N    P    V
3.  Although I was absent for a month, I finished the
       N               N
    semester with good grades.
```

4. When the lights went out, she looked for candles.
   - N: lights, she, candles
   - V: went, looked
   - P: for

5. Drivers must pass a new test every ten years, or they may not drive.
   - N: Drivers, test, years, they
   - V: must pass, may not drive
   - P: or

EXERCISE 3, p. 131

The sentences are sample answers.

1. Noun.
   The car landed on its roof.
2. Noun and verb.
   The label bore a poison warning. [Noun.] The companies must label their products. [Verb.]
3. Noun.
   The door flew open by itself.
4. Noun.
   My younger sister was good company.
5. Noun and verb.
   The whistle released us from work. . [Noun.] We whistle all the way home. [Verb.]
6. Noun and verb.
   We are getting into condition for the meet. [Noun.]
   We condition our muscles with weightlifting. [Verb.]
7. Noun and verb.
   I can still hear the sing of the bullet. [Noun.]
   The children sing softly. [Verb.]
8. Noun and verb.
   The post stood upright. [Noun.] Please post this letter. [Verb.]
9. Noun.
   The attic became a playroom.
10. Noun and verb.
    the glue stuck to my hands. [Noun.] We glue our models together. [Verb.]

EXERCISE 4, p. 134

1. Calls is transitive.
   Marie calls her boyfriend a genius.
   - DO: boyfriend
   - OC: genius

2. <u>Was</u> is linking.
                                    SC
   The dentist's bill was five hundred <u>dollars</u>.
3. <u>Find</u> is transitive.
                      DO   OC
   Many adults find rock <u>concerts</u> <u>strange</u>.
4. <u>Read</u> is transitive.
              IO   DO
   I read my <u>brother</u> <u>Charlotte's Web</u>.
5. <u>Bought</u> is transitive.
              IO   DO
   Then I bought <u>him</u> his own <u>copy</u>.
6. <u>Is</u> is linking.
                            SC
   Moderate exercise is <u>good</u> for your heart.
7. <u>Argued</u> is intransitive.
   No objects or complements.
8. <u>Was</u> is linking.
                          SC
   The counterfeiter was a <u>child</u>.
9. <u>Proclaimed</u> is transitive.
                              DO   OC
   The newspapers proclaimed the <u>election</u> an <u>upset</u>.
10. <u>Showed</u> is transitive.
                        IO   DO
    The magician showed the <u>audience</u> his <u>tricks</u>.

EXERCISE 5, p. 135

Sample answers:

1. Josie caught the ball.
2. My uncle brought me a cake.
3. Matthew cried.
4. Sometimes they think themselves very unlucky.
5. Marilou seems unhappy.
6. One candidate called the other a crook.
7. We became reckless.
8. Thousands of witnesses watched the murder.
9. We bought ourselves a television set.
10. No one studied.

EXERCISE 6, p. 136

1. The <u>icy</u> rain created <u>glassy</u> patches on the roads.
   ADJ   ADJ
Sample imitation: The blue bird turned graceful circles in the air.

2. <u>Happily</u>, children used the <u>slippery</u> streets as playgrounds.
   ADV   ADJ
Sample imitation: Quickly, we slipped the large key in the lock.

3. <u>Fortunately</u>, <u>no</u> cars ventured <u>out</u>.
   ADV   ADJ   ADV
Sample imitation: Impatiently, the old man gazed ahead.

4. <u>Wise</u> parents stayed <u>indoors</u> where they would be <u>warm</u> and <u>dry</u>.
   ADJ   ADV   ADJ
Sample imitation: Smart children go outdoors when they feel noisy and rambunctious.

5. The dogs slept <u>soundly</u> near the <u>warm</u> radiators, <u>seldom</u> going <u>outside</u>.
                ADV   ADJ   ADV
Sample imitation: The babies lay quietly in their small cribs, rarely yelling aloud.

EXERCISE 7, p. 137

The sentences are sample answers.

1. watchfully
   The tiger was <u>watchful</u>.   The sailor peered <u>watchfully</u> into the gloom.
2. wise
   The minister spoke <u>wisely</u> to the congregation.   The <u>wise</u> child knows its own parent.
3. newly
   The <u>new</u> book smelled of wood.   The <u>newly</u> planted petunias wilted in the sun.
4. brightly
   The <u>bright</u> colors were unflattering.   The sun glinted <u>brightly</u> off the tin roof.
5. fortunate
   <u>Fortunately</u>, I passed the test.   We are <u>fortunate</u> to be living in these times.

6. even
   The cards were _evenly_ distributed. The seamstress made
   the hem _even_.
7. happily
   Two _happy_ people left the church. The child skipped
   happily along the street.
8. painful
   She spoke _painfully_. It was a _painful_ decision.
9. dark
   My aunt glowered _darkly_ at me. _Dark_ clouds warned of a
   storm.
10. sturdily
   The _sturdy_ table was fifty years old. The little boy
   faced the dog _sturdily_.

EXERCISE 8, p. 138

Sample answers:

1. The _typed manuscript_ contained many errors.
2. _Painted birds_ decorate the window.
3. He wanted to know the origins of the _written word_.
4. The _burned house_ was a shock.
5. The _pitching boat_ almost foundered.
6. The man escaped the _charging animal_.
7. We picked the _ripened fruit_.
8. The dinghy tossed on _rolling waves_.
9. All the _known facts_ contradict his theory.
10. _Driven people_ may have hypertension.

EXERCISE 9, p. 138

Possible answers:

1. The trembling shadows made the evening spooky.
2. The frightened dog barked loudly.
3. A careful driver can avoid unhappy accidents.
4. Growing children leave behind many broken toys.
5. The blustery wind invited flying kites.
6. The wrecked car is a silver Chevrolet.
7. We recently bought our father a carving knife.
8. The brass doors open inward.
9. The deep oceans contain peculiar fish.
10. The lisping boy spoke softly.

EXERCISE 10, p. 140

          ⌐ADJ   ⌐ADV   ⌐ADJ
The woman in blue socks ran from the policeman on horseback.
   ⌐ADV   ⌐ADV
She darted down Bates Street and then into the bus depot.
ADV⎯⎯⎯⎯⎯⎯⎯⎯⎯⎯⎯⎯⎯⎯⎯⎯⎯⎯⎯   ⌐ADV
At the depot the policeman dismounted from his horse and
   ⌐ADV   ⌐ADJ
searched for the woman. The entrance to the depot and the inte-
       ⌐ADV   ADV⎯⎯⎯⎯⎯⎯⎯
rior were filled with travelers, however, and in the crowd he lost
  ⌐ADJ   ⌐ADJ
sight of the woman. She, meanwhile, had boarded a bus on the
    ⌐ADJ   ⌐ADV
other side of the depot and was riding across town.

EXERCISE 11, p. 141

Possible answers:

1. The band members held a party for one hundred people.
2. Tiny minnows swim in the small pond.
3. We are required to write the exam in pencil on white paper.
4. The monkey with silver fur chattered noisily.
5. The interview continued for two hours.
6. Jan received a glass paperweight from an unknown admirer.
7. They took a long walk along the stream and across the bridge.
8. The wagging tail of a dog toppled the lamp.
9. The author wants to shock readers with foul language and gruesome crimes.
10. Everyone except Vicky and Carlos attended the lecture.

EXERCISE 12, p. 144

          ADJ
1. Defeated at Waterloo, Napoleon was sent into exile.
                     ⌐⎯⎯ADV⎯⎯   ADJ
2. We must be strong enough to face the death of loved ones.
   ADJ   ADJ
3. Whimpering and moaning, my brother was finally dragged
      ADV
to be vaccinated.

139

                          N   ADJ
4. Eating at a nice restaurant is a relaxing way
     ⌐ADJ   ADJ   ⌐
    to end a demanding week.
          N   ADJ
5. To fly was one of humankind's recurring dreams.
         ADJ   ⌐   ADJ   ⌐N
6. The dwindling water supply made the remaining vacationers
                            N
    decide to leave for another campground.

    [The infinitive phrase the . . . campground is the DO of
    the verb made. The infinitive phrase to . . . campground
    is the object of the infinitive decide.]
                                                      N
7. The hungry wolves were kept at bay by the periodic firing

    of a rifle.
                              ⌐   N   ADJ
8. The train moved too fast for us to enjoy the passing

    countryside.
                          N
9. After missing church three times in a row, I received a

    call from the minister.
            ADJ   ADJ
10. Three misbehaving children ruined our attempt to stage

    a play in the elementary school.

EXERCISE 13, p. 144

Possible answers:

1. Falling far behind the other runners, Lee knew she had
    lost the race.
2. Convicted of two burglaries, the teenager spent six months
    in reform school.
3. The letter, opened by mistake, was lying on the table.
4. Having found his wallet, Bobby could buy his books.
5. The giraffe's long neck is essential for reaching leaves
    and bark high in trees.
6. Shopping in supermarkets with their parents is an early
    experience almost all children share.
7. I must get a job to support myself.

8. The retired couple used their free time well, traveling across the country and back several times.
9. Cleaning the cellar, they discovered a box of old money.
10. By jogging every day for a month, I have lost five pounds.

EXERCISE 14, p. 145

Possible answers:

1. Her face turning pale, she stared at the woman ahead of her.
2. The steelworkers having called a strike, the factory was closed down.
3. We were forced to cancel the annual picnic, the funds having run out.
4. The thief stood before the safe, his fingers twitching eagerly.
5. His arms thrashing, the swimmer rose again to the surface.

EXERCISE 15, p. 148

                                                          ADV
1. The auctioneer opened the bidding when everyone was seated.
                          N (object of preposition)
2. They were unperturbed by what the strange man screamed

   at them.
                     ADV
3. Whenever the economy is uncertain, people tend to become

   more selfish.
                N (subject)
4. Whoever wants to graduate must pass all the required

   courses.
                                              ADV
5. I knew the ending would be unhappy when the main character

   started falling apart.
                 N (subject)
6. That Stefanie did not go to college was a disappointment

   to her parents.

                                    ADV
7. Ever since she was a small child, they have saved money

   for her education.
                                    N (direct object)
8. Stefanie decided, though, that she wanted to work a year

   or two before college.
                         ADV
9. Until she makes up her mind, Stefanie's education money

   is collecting interest.
                                         ADJ
10. Her parents are the kind who let their children think for

    themselves.

EXERCISE 16, p. 149

Possible answers:

1. The hunter tried to move the stone, which was very
   heavy.
2. We came to the gate where we had first seen the deer
   tracks.
3. Someone who is fickle cannot be relied on.
4. The fact that Abner won the award still amazes us.
5. When the town government canceled the new playground,
   small children demonstrated in the streets.
6. You should know that we can make no exceptions.
7. Those dogs have a master who gives them equal discipline
   and praise.
8. Although the basketball team has had a losing season, the
   team shows promise.
9. He did not bother to undress for bed because he was too
   tired.
10. She is the teacher who gives very few A's.

EXERCISE 17, p. 150

Possible answers:

1. Jerry's aim, to avoid all productive labor, will surely
   change when his parents stop supporting him.

2. Their Beatles memorabilia--records, photographs, posters, and T-shirts--occupied a room in their basement.
3. The little boy, a nasty, spoiled brat, cannot be left alone with other children.
4. Cactus growing, a hobby with no immediate rewards, attracts patient people.
5. The most popular professional team sports--football, baseball, basketball, and hockey--pay their players well.
6. Edgar Allan Poe, a writer of fantastic, scary stories, was also a poet and a journalist.
7. The radio talk show received a call from Warren Jones, the escaped prisoner.
8. The house, a five-room adobe structure, was bought by a neighborhood group.
9. The hailstorm hit at 5:30, the height of rush hour.
10. English adopted many words for animals, such as <u>moose</u>, <u>opossum</u>, and <u>raccoon</u>, from the Algonquin Indians.

EXERCISE 18, p. 154

Possible answers:

1. Geoffrey raked some leaves <u>but</u> stopped before he had finished the job.
2. <u>Either</u> television news will have to get better, <u>or</u> I <u>might</u> give up news programs for newspapers.
3. Physics is a difficult <u>but</u> enjoyable subject.
4. The football team's morale was bad; <u>moreover</u>, the team had a losing season.
5. The cheerleaders <u>and</u> the back-up center missed the bus.
6. Politicians cannot be shy people; <u>indeed</u>, they must be outgoing.
7. The newspaper publishes interesting feature articles; <u>however</u>, it publishes feeble editorials.
8. The pelicans floated on the smooth water <u>and</u> sometimes dipped beneath the surface to catch fish.
9. <u>Both</u> my mother <u>and</u> my mother-in-law attended Thomas Jefferson High School.
10. The news stories from Uganda were censored; <u>furthermore</u>, they were out-of-date because the censor held on to them for so long.

143

EXERCISE 19, p. 156

Sample answers:

1. <u>Will</u> the <u>water boil</u>?
   <u>Boil</u> the <u>water</u>, please.
2. <u>Did</u> the <u>music stop</u>?
   <u>Stop</u> the <u>music</u>.
3. <u>Have</u> you <u>set</u> the <u>table</u>?
   <u>Set</u> the <u>table</u>.
4. <u>Will</u> someone <u>write</u> on the <u>blackboard</u>?
   <u>Write</u> on the <u>blackboard</u>.
5. Who <u>can use</u> the <u>telephone</u>?
   <u>Use</u> the <u>telephone</u>.

EXERCISE 20, p. 157

1. The <u>quarterback threw</u> the football for more than forty yards.
2. <u>Whether microwave ovens are dangerous is</u> uncertain.
3. The plane <u>crash killed</u> sixty people.
4. The pilot's <u>skill saved</u> the lives of over one hundred others.
5. An <u>audience</u> of nearly ten thousand <u>was</u> at the concert.

EXERCISE 21, p. 159

1. Simple: ⌐————INDEPENDENT————⌐
   Winters in Vermont are beautiful.
2. Simple: ⌐—————INDEPENDENT—————
   Summers in Vermont, by the way, are no less
   beautiful.
3. Complex: ⌐————— SUBORDINATE —————⌐
   Although the guest of honor arrived late,
   ⌐—INDEPENDENT—⌐
   no one seemed to mind.
4. Compound: ⌐————INDEPENDENT————⌐
   The police strike lasted a week, but
   ⌐————INDEPENDENT————⌐
   no robberies occurred in that time.

5. Compound-complex:
```
                         ┌─────────SUBORDINATE ─────────
5.  Compound-complex:    Even though some say football has
```
```
                                                    ┌──────────
    supplanted baseball as the national pastime, millions of
    ┌───────────INDEPENDENT───────────┐   ┌──INDEPENDENT──────
    people watch baseball every year and they don't seem ready
```
```
    ┌──────┐
    to stop.
```

EXERCISE 22, p. 159

Possible answers:

1. Dinner was tasty, but it did not fill us up.
2. Although the storm was predicted to be fierce, it passed
    by quickly.
3. When the musical notes died away, a strange object filled
    the sky.
4. The wolves were afraid of the fire.
5. We hoped that the rumors would stop, but they did not.

Chapter 6   Case of Nouns and Pronouns

EXERCISE 1, p. 163

1.	he	5.	he	8.	I
2.	me	6.	him and me	9.	I
3.	they	7.	she	10.	me
4.	me				

EXERCISE 2, p. 164

1.	us	4.	she
2.	us	5.	us, me
3.	We		

EXERCISE 3, p. 166

1.	Who	5.	Who	8.	whom
2.	Whoever	6.	who	9.	whoever
3.	whom	7.	whoever	10.	whom
4.	Whom				

145

EXERCISE 4, p. 167

Possible answers:

1. Children who have problems seeing or hearing may do
    poorly in school.
2. Carolyn knows the person whom we invited to speak.
3. The woman who wrote that letter must have been angry.
4. David is the candidate who we think deserves to win.
5. Truman was a president whom my father greatly admired.

EXERCISE 5, p. 168

> After class Tom and I [subject] drove to the ware-
house to pick up Tom's trunk. Between him and me [objects
of preposition], we [subject] could just lift the trunk's
lid. We [subject] looked around for someone who [subject]
could help us [direct object], someone whom [object of
verb and preposition count on] we [subject] could count on
to supply extra muscle. The man we [subject] found proved
no stronger than we [subject of clause in comparison], but
his [possessive before gerund] pulling and our [possessive
before gerund] pushing were enough to get the trunk on a
dolly and into our [possessive] car. We [subject] left
him [object of verb and subject of infinitive] to help
the next weaklings who [subject] showed up.

Chapter 7   Verb Forms, Tense, Mood, and Voice

EXERCISE 1, p. 173

1. Every afternoon after work, we have swum at the city pool
    and then held a party. [Both past participles.]
2. The minister spoke to the Kiwanis Club last night. [Past
    tense.]
3. Because the day was so dark, it seemed as though the sun
    had never risen. [Past participle.]
4. Before we could stop him, my cousin had drunk all the
    chocolate milk and had eaten all the cookies. [Both past
    participles.]
5. The fans were encouraged because their team had not lost
    a game all season. [Past participle.]

6. She <u>kept</u> hoping she would be <u>chosen</u> for the lacrosse team. [Past tense and past participle.]
7. The wind <u>blew</u>, ˅and my hands almost <u>froze</u>. [Both past tense.]
8. If we had not <u>left</u> the table, we would have <u>fallen</u> asleep. [Both past participles.]
9. The dry spell was <u>broken</u> when the rains <u>began</u> again. [Past participle and past tense.]
10. The halfback <u>caught</u> the pass <u>thrown</u> by the quarterback. [Past tense and past participle.]

EXERCISE 2, p. 174

1. The spider <u>sat</u> in its web and <u>lay</u> in wait for its prey.
2. After she had <u>set</u> the table, she <u>lay</u> a cloth over it.
3. Joan's wallet had <u>lain</u> in the street for two days.
4. The skunk <u>lay</u> asleep in the trap.
5. He <u>lay</u> the sick child down for a nap and then <u>sat</u> watching over her.

EXERCISE 3, p. 175

A teacher sometimes <u>asks</u> too much of a student. In high school I was once <u>punished</u> for being sick. I had <u>missed</u> some school, and I <u>realized</u> that I would fail a test unless I had a chance to <u>make</u> up the class work. I <u>discussed</u> the problem with the teacher, but he said I was <u>supposed</u> to make up the work while I was sick. At that I <u>walked</u> out of the class. I <u>received</u> a failing grade then, but it did not change my attitudes. Today I still balk when a teacher <u>makes</u> unreasonable demands or <u>expects</u> too much.

EXERCISE 4, p. 180

1. My grandfather died before I <u>arrived</u> at the hospital. <u>Or:</u> My grandfather <u>had died</u> before I <u>arrived</u> at the hospital.
2. The jury recommends leniency because the criminal <u>is</u> so young. <u>Or:</u> The jury <u>recommended</u> leniency because the criminal was so young.
3. The mechanic would have liked <u>to own</u> the car. <u>Or:</u> The mechanic <u>would like</u> to have owned the car.
4. The archaeologist opened the tomb when the bats inside it <u>were</u> killed.

5. She <u>has been</u> on the critical list since she fell yester-day.
6. The stagehands refused to put up the set for the play be-cause they <u>thought</u> the design <u>was</u> unsafe. <u>Or:</u> The stage-hands <u>refuse</u> to put up the set for the play because they think the design is unsafe.
7. Many shopkeeprs should have done more <u>to protect</u> them-selves against robberies.
8. I enroll only in courses that <u>leave</u> me time to work. <u>Or:</u> I <u>enrolled</u> only in courses that left me time to work.
9. <u>Driving</u> without my glasses on, I caused an accident. <u>Or:</u> <u>Having driven</u> without my glasses on, I <u>had caused</u> an acci-dent.
10. The police claimed that the dog <u>bit</u> the child.

EXERCISE 5, p. 180

1. Everyone who <u>auditioned</u> for the play <u>was</u> (or <u>will be</u>) given a part.
2. I <u>would have liked</u> <u>to attend</u> that concert.
3. The elderly man <u>hopes</u> that his children <u>will visit</u> him over Chanukah.
4. Soldiers <u>were taught</u> to obey commands so that their nerves <u>would be</u> steady during combat.
5. Everyone <u>believes</u> the woman <u>is</u> crazy because she repeatedly <u>claims</u> she <u>has seen</u> a ghost.

EXERCISE 6, p. 183

1. If I <u>were</u> happier, I would not have so much trouble in school.
2. Marie asks that the motion <u>be</u> adopted.
3. The syllabus requires that each student <u>write</u> three papers and <u>take</u> two essay tests.
4. They treat me as if I <u>were</u> their son.
5. If a road <u>were</u> connecting them, the two towns could do business with each other.

EXERCISE 7, p. 184

1. <u>Doctors</u> often <u>prescribe</u> drugs to relieve depression.
2. Foreign fishing <u>fleets</u> still <u>kill</u> whales.
3. Over thirty <u>people were killed</u> by the plane crash.
4. A passing <u>freighter discovered</u> the survivors.

5. The people of the Middle Ages thought the Church very important.

EXERCISE 8, p. 184

We used to know nothing about our earliest ancestors. Before Darwin's On the Origin of Species was published in 1859, people thought humans were only thousands of years old. Now we know that the earliest animals to walk upright on two legs (a sign of being human) existed millions of years ago. Anthropologists in Africa discovered footprints almost like ours that are 3½ million years old. When the footprints were excavated, they were seen to be lying beside the remains of an ancient river that had long since dried up.

Chapter 8   Agreement

EXERCISE 1, p. 193

1. A number of students were seen among the demonstrators.
2. Neither that drawing nor those paintings appeal to my friend.
3. Margaret Gayoso is among those who are going to Washington to lobby for preservation of the wilderness.
4. The idea that the college should grant privileges to athletes is ridiculous.
5. Sentence correct.
6. Surely someone among all those experts knows the answer.
7. Mathematics is his special problem.
8. Seminars has a more elegant sound than classes.
9. Sentence correct.
10. The police claimed that the crowd was endangering public safety.

11. He is one of those persons who <u>break</u> promises easily.
12. Sentence correct.
13. Neither the chemistry instructor nor her lab assistants <u>seem</u> to know the assignment for today.
14. A new porch door, in addition to new windows, <u>is</u> needed.
15. Either the manager or his representative <u>is</u> responsible for handling complaints.

EXERCISE 2, p. 196

1. Each of the fifty parents visited <u>his or her</u> child's teacher. <u>Or:</u> <u>All parents</u> visited <u>their children's teachers</u>.
2. Sentence correct.
3. Everyone on the women's basketball team brought <u>her</u> own equipment.
4. No new parent feels entirely secure in <u>his or her</u> role. <u>Or:</u> New <u>parents never feel</u> entirely secure in their role.
5. The team had never won on <u>its</u> home court.
6. The town offers few opportunities for someone to let out <u>his</u> (or his or her) tensions. <u>Or:</u> The town offers few opportunities for <u>people</u> to let out their tensions.
7. Each of the thirty students conducted <u>his</u> (or his or her) own experiments. <u>Or:</u> <u>All thirty students</u> conducted their own experiments.
8. Will either Mary or Lucy send in <u>her application</u>? <u>Or:</u> Will <u>Mary and Lucy</u> send in their applications?
9. Sentence correct.
10. Did any of the boys believe <u>he</u> would get away with cheating? <u>Or:</u> Did <u>the boys</u> believe they would get away with cheating?

EXERCISE 3, p. 196

1. <u>People</u> who <u>do</u> poorly in school often <u>lose</u> respect for <u>themselves</u>.
2. A <u>teen-ager</u> who <u>collects</u> baseball cards often <u>devotes</u> much time and money to <u>his</u> (or his or her) hobby.
3. <u>Dancers</u> who <u>fail</u> to practice <u>risk</u> injuring <u>themselves</u>.
4. The <u>computer was</u> purchased because of <u>its</u> simplicity.
5. <u>His</u> (or <u>Her</u>) exams over, the <u>senior celebrated</u> by throwing a party.
6. The <u>photograph shows</u> the beauty of the landscape, but <u>its</u> dim light obscures details.

7. <u>Each worker</u> has some complaint about <u>his</u> (or <u>her</u> or <u>his</u> <u>or her</u>) job.
8. Even though the disarmament <u>conference</u> <u>has</u> resulted in little change, the government continues to attend <u>it</u>.
9. <u>Judith and Bill</u> <u>are</u> the <u>ones</u> who always <u>make</u> the decisions, and the rest of us resent <u>their</u> authority.
10. Since we don't know what's behind <u>them</u>, the locked <u>doors</u> <u>seem</u> more mysterious than <u>they</u> probably <u>are</u>.

EXERCISE 4, p. 197

Everyone has <u>his</u> (or <u>his or her</u>) favorite view of professional athletes. A common view is that the athletes are like well-paid children who have no real work to do, have no responsibilities, and simply enjoy the game and the good money. But this view of professional athletes <u>fails</u> to consider the grueling training the athletes have to go through to become professionals. Either training or competing <u>leads</u> each athlete to take risks that can result in <u>his</u> (or <u>his or her</u>) serious injury. The athletes have tremendous responsibility to the team they play on, which <u>needs</u> to function as a unit at all times to win <u>its</u> games. Most athletes are finished as active team players by the age of forty, when <u>they are</u> too stiff and banged-up to go on. Rather than just listening to any of the people who <u>criticize</u> professional athletes, everyone interested in sports <u>needs</u> to defend the athletes. They take stiff physical punishment so neither the sports fanatic nor the casual observer <u>is</u> deprived of <u>his</u> (or <u>his or her</u>) pleasure.

Chapter 9   <u>Adjectives and Adverbs</u>

EXERCISE 1, p. 201

```
        ADV ──→ V              ADJ ──→ N
```
1. The demonstrators <u>quickly</u> dispersed when the <u>local</u> police arrived.
   Sample imitation: The children quietly giggled when the red-haired clown wept.
```
           V              ADJ ──→ N      ──ADV
```
2. Everyone in the class answered the <u>hardest</u> question <u>wrong</u>.
   Sample imitation: Somebody in the crowd yelled a rude remark loudly.

```
          ADJ        ADJ        N              PRON        ADJ
```
3. He was <u>such</u> an <u>exciting</u> person that everyone felt <u>bad</u>
    when he left.
    Sample imitation: Susan is such an energetic woman that
    anyone seems lazy in comparison.
```
     ADV      ADJ      N                    ADJ      N
```
4. Even <u>in good weather</u>, one of the <u>surest</u> ways to cause an
    ```
              V        ADJ     N    ADV    ADV
    ```
    accident is to follow <u>another</u> car <u>too</u> <u>closely</u>.
    Sample imitation: Even at exam time, one of the best ways
    to study a subject is to organize the material very
    thoroughly.
    ```
        ADJ       N      ADV      V     Verbal            ADV
    ```
5. As the <u>Ferris</u> wheel <u>slowly</u> turned, raising him <u>higher</u> in
    ```
        PRON              ADV        ADJ
    ```
    the air, he became <u>increasingly</u> <u>ill</u>.
    Sample imitation: When the gray dog loudly barked, baring
    his teeth menacingly, I felt strangely unafraid.

EXERCISE 2, p. 201

1. I was <u>really</u> surprised when Martin and Emily got a divorce.
2. If you practice the piano <u>regularly</u>, you will soon be
    able to play real music.
3. Sentence correct.
4. After playing <u>poorly</u> for six games, the hockey team
    finally had a game that was good.
5. If people learned karate, they could stop would-be rob-
    bers <u>quickly</u>, before the robbers could steal anything.

EXERCISE 3, p. 204

The sentences are sample answers.

1. interesting, more interesting, most interesting
    The book was <u>interesting</u>. It was <u>more interesting</u>
    than the movie. It was one of the <u>most interesting</u> books
    I have ever read.
2. great, greater, greatest
    A <u>great</u> tremor shook the earth. The tremor was <u>greater</u>
    than the earlier one. The <u>greatest</u> tremor was still to
    come.
3. lively, livelier, liveliest
    The children were <u>lively</u> yesterday. They are <u>livelier</u>
    today. The <u>liveliest</u> child sets the pattern for the
    others.

4. hasty, hastier, hastiest
   <u>Hasty</u> decisions rarely turn out well. Our departure was <u>hastier</u> than it should have been. Sam made the <u>hastiest</u> exit I've ever seen.
5. some, more, most
   <u>Some</u> apples are in the basket. <u>More</u> apples are in the cooler. <u>Most</u> apples are red or green.
6. often, more often, most often
   We do not see our grandparents <u>often</u>. We would like to see them <u>more often</u>. <u>Most often</u>, we see our aunts and uncles.
7. good, better, best
   The fruit tasted <u>good</u>. The cheese tasted <u>better</u>. The chocolate pie tasted <u>best</u>.
8. well, better, best
   Julie did <u>well</u> on the test. Jack did <u>better</u> than Julie. Ellen did <u>best</u> of all.
9. majestic, more majestic, most majestic
   The <u>majestic</u> ceremony impressed the crowd. The older prince's demeanor was <u>more majestic</u> than his brother's. The <u>most majestic</u> carriage was the queen's.
10. badly, worse, worst
    The favored horse performed <u>badly</u> in the race. He performed <u>worse</u> than all but one other horse. The horse that performed <u>worst</u> broke stride and left the race.

EXERCISE 4, p. 204

1. If I study hard, I should be able to do <u>better</u> on the next economics test.
2. Working last summer as an assistant to my congressman was a <u>unique</u> experience.
3. My uncle is the <u>youngest</u> of three brothers.
4. He was the <u>cruelest</u> person I ever met.
5. Of the two major problems with nuclear power plants-- waste disposal and radiation leakage--radiation leakage is the <u>more</u> terrifying.

EXERCISE 5, p. 205

1. She and her sisters argued over which of them was <u>the smartest</u>.
2. The <u>university administration's policy on student absenteeism</u> was controversial.

3. He rehearsed long enough to do <u>really</u> well in his audition for a part in the play, but he was too scared to speak <u>loudly</u> enough.

4. Jerry was not more mature than his brother, though he was <u>older</u>.

5. As we huddled over our sick guinea pig, he seemed to grow <u>more nearly dead</u> by the hour.

6. The food tasted so <u>bad</u> that we were certain we would feel <u>strange</u> or worse in the morning.

7. Sentence correct.

8. One can buy a tape player <u>cheaply</u>, but the cheap players rarely work <u>well</u> or last long.

9. Jessica spoke <u>carefully</u> and <u>calmly</u> to ensure that she would be understood.

10. Doors open <u>easily</u> in dry weather.

Part III

CLEAR SENTENCES

Chapter 10   Sentence Fragments

EXERCISE 1, p. 210

Possible answers:

1. I enjoy New England more in the winter than in the summer, especially now that I have learned to ski.
2. Freshman English is not as difficult as people say, unless someone is not willing to do the work.
3. No sentence fragment.
4. Whenever they lose touch with their children, parents blame themselves.
5. The judgments of movie critics are often unreliable. They look for qualities that many people do not care about.

EXERCISE 2, p. 212

Possible answers:

1. Being both exciting and dangerous, drag racing is a mixed pleasure.
2. By engaging people in things outside their work, a hobby can be important to a fulfilling life.
3. Just to stay awake is the major challenge of long-distance driving.
4. The flag was whipping back and forth in the wind. It made a frightening sound.
5. No sentence fragment.

EXERCISE 3, p. 212

Possible answers:

1. The gun was where the police expected to find it, in a garbage can behind the movie theater.
2. No sentence fragment.
3. The house will take at least three weeks to paint, even with two painters working full-time.
4. This weekend we discovered a new leak under the house in a space occupied by some rodents that had decided to live with us.
5. In moving heavy things, you should be careful to lift using your legs, not your back.

EXERCISE 4, p. 214

Possible answers:

1. During World War II Jack Armstrong, the all-American boy, was a hero for young people.
2. Lynn graduated from college in 1982 and spent six months trying to find a job.
3. The college of business administration offers several degrees and the opportunity to be an intern for one of many businesses.
4. In whatever form--whether cigarettes, cigars, pipe tobacco, or chewing tobacco--tobacco is bad for one's health.
5. No sentence fragment.

EXERCISE 5, p. 215

Possible answers:

1. The drunken driver swerved across the cement median strip. Then he hit four parked cars in a row.
2. Classes may not resume after vacation. The school has run out of money.
3. The child appeared at the hospital. He was badly beaten and abandoned by his parents.
4. An unknown person gave the acting company an old building. He or she also gave the money to convert the building to a theater.
5. The old photograph shows a handsome man. He holds himself stiffly so as not to blur the image.

EXERCISE 6, p. 215

Possible revision:

> Becoming an adult can mean moving into the best
> years of life or moving downhill from the "high" of ado-
> lescence. <u>Which it is depends</u> on one's outlook<u>, on one</u>'s
> experiences as a child, and one's view of adulthood. Be-
> ginning at about age twenty, people enter a new world.
> Released from the restrictions adults place on them<u>, they</u>
> are approaching their physical and mental peak. The
> world is ahead<u>, waiting</u> to challenge and be challenged.
> If their experiences as children have made them secure
> with themselves and others, they may welcome the chal-
> lenges of adulthood. But those challenges can also seem
> frightening and overwhelming <u>if</u> childhood and adolescence
> have already presented too many battles to figh<u>t and t</u>oo
> little security.

Chapter 11   <u>Comma Splices and Run-on Sentences</u>

EXERCISE 1, p. 221

Possible answers:

1. a. The election was held on a rainy day, <u>and</u> the weather
   kept people away from the polls.
   b. The election was held on a rainy day.<u> The</u> weather
   kept people away from the polls.
2. a. <u>Although</u> my brother enlisted in the Marines for three
   years, he will probably reenlist when his hitch is up.
   b. My brother enlisted in the Marines for three years,
   <u>but</u> he will probably reenlist when his hitch is up.
3. No comma splice.
4. a. Marian never seems to stop, <u>for</u> she has so much energy.
   b. Marian never seems to stop<u>;</u> she has so much energy.
5. a. Snow fell for three days in a row<u>;</u> consequently<u>,</u> the
   superintendent had to shut down the school.
   b. Snow fell for three days in a row.<u> Consequently,</u> the
   superintendent had to shut down the school.
6. a. <u>Even though</u> Sean bought a new suit for the interview,
   he didn't get the job.
   b. Sean bought a new suit for the interview, <u>but</u> he
   didn't get the job.

7. a. Little Orphan Annie used to be just a comic-strip
    character; now, however, she has become a character in a
    musical.
    b. Little Orphan Annie used to be just a comic-strip
    character. Now, however, she has become a character in
    a musical.
8. a. Politicians rarely deal squarely with complex issues
    because they are too worried about alienating potential
    supporters.
    b. Politicians rarely deal squarely with complex issues;
    they are too worried about alienating potential supporters.
9. a. Many home owners are rebelling against property taxes
    because they believe they should not have to bear the ex-
    pense of local government.
    b. Many home owners are rebelling against property
    taxes. They believe they should not have to bear the
    expense of local government.
10. a. The apartment has an excellent view, but it looks out
    over a parking lot at the expansive town dump.
    b. The apartment has an excellent view; it looks out
    over a parking lot at the expansive town dump.

EXERCISE 2, p. 222

Possible answers:

1. a. The rain fell so hard that water started pouring into
    the kitchen from the back porch, and it blew around the
    kitchen windows too.
    b. The rain fell so hard that water started pouring into
    the kitchen from the back porch. It blew around the
    kitchen windows too.
2. a. Children sometimes misbehave just to test their
    elders, and parents should discipline them on those
    occasions.
    b. When children misbehave just to test their elders,
    parents should discipline them.
3. a. Although the skills center offers job training to
    people who need it, the center can't guarantee jobs.
    b. The skills center offers job training to people who
    need it. The center can't guarantee jobs, though.
4. a. Because the parking problem in the downtown area is
    getting out of hand, the mayor suggests a new under-
    ground parking garage.
    b. The parking problem in the downtown area is getting
    out of hand, so the mayor suggests a new underground
    parking garage.

5. a. Science courses teach interesting content; they also
        teach one to think logically about the world.
    b. Science courses teach interesting content. They also
        teach one to think logically about the world.

EXERCISE 3, p. 222

Possible answers:

1. I once worked as a switchboard operator; however, after
    a week I was fired for hopeless incompetence.
2. When the candidate's backers learned of his previous
    illegal activities, they withdrew their support.
3. Record prices stayed stable for a long time, but they
    rose sharply in the last decade.
4. Teachers sometimes make unfair assignments because they
    don't take account of the workload in other courses.
5. I nearly froze trying to unlock the car door; then I dis-
    covered I was standing next to the wrong red Rabbit.
6. Many proud people restrict their activities because they
    are afraid to fail at something new.
7. We thought my seven-year-old brother was a genius when
    he read an entire encyclopedia.
8. The driver was lucky to escape uninjured; his car was
    destroyed, however.
9. Some Eskimos found and nursed the sick explorer, but he
    died two weeks later.
10. Two railroad lines cut through the town, and they inter-
    sect a block from the main street.

EXERCISE 4, p. 223

Possible revision:

    A pleasant, inexpensive treat is a weekend in a
country inn. Inns are usually located in quaint, quiet
villages. There is little noise during the night except
for crickets, and the surrounding area is countryside,
often with historical sites to visit. The innkeeper is
sometimes a great cook. I have had delicious breakfasts
at inns, and frequently they are included in the charge
for the room. The rooms themselves are large and airy,
the chairs are soft, and the beds are just right. The
trip to the inn may take an hour, and the weekend may
cost no more than twenty dollars. It's a great break
from school or work. I recommend it to everyone.

Chapter 12   <u>Pronoun Reference</u>

EXERCISE 1, p. 226

Possible answers:

1. If your pet cheetah will not eat raw meat, cook <u>the meat</u>.
2. Did and his cousin did not get along because <u>Dick</u> (or <u>his cousin</u>) liked to have his own way.
3. Since Bill had been driving the car that rolled into the truck, he is responsible for the damage to <u>the car</u> (or <u>the truck</u>).
4. My father and his sister have not spoken for thirty years because she left the family when my grandfather was ill and never called or wrote. But now <u>my father</u> is thinking of resuming communication.
5. <u>In the rotting shed</u> Saul found an old gun that was just as his grandfather had left it.
6. There is a difference between the heroes of today and the heroes of yesterday: <u>Today's heroes</u> have flaws in their characters.
7. Jan held the sandwich in one hand and the telephone in the other, eating <u>the sandwich</u> while she talked.
8. <u>To take the photograph,</u> she used a camera that had been in her family since the 1920s.
9. Tom told his brother, "<u>I am</u> (or <u>You are</u>) in trouble at home."
10. Denver was where my grandmother grew up. The city had been the scene of a mad gold rush with fortune seekers, plush opera houses, makeshift hotels, noisy saloons, and dirt streets. When I was a child, <u>my grandmother</u> often retold the stories she had heard of those days.

EXERCISE 2, p. 231

Possible answers:

1. We receive warnings to beware of nuclear fallout, pesticides, smog, and oil shortages, but I try not to think about <u>those dangers</u>.
2. In <u>his</u> novels <u>F. Scott Fitzgerald</u> write about the Jazz Age.
3. By the time the firemen arrived at the scene, <u>the fire</u> was blazing out of control.

4. Carl is a master carpenter because his father, a cabinet-maker, taught him about carpentry when Carl was a teen-ager.
5. Partly because the title character is a complicated and ambiguous hero, Macbeth is a good play.
6. After hearing Professor Eakins's lecture on marine biology, I think I want to become a marine biologist.
7. Urban redevelopment projects are attempts to make neighborhoods safe and attractive.
8. The nineteenth century didn't offer many options in motorized transportation.
9. My car Harriet, which has no roof, is useless when it rains.
10. We hoped we had a winning lottery ticket so that we could pay the debt, but winning was not something we could count on.
11. Few people dare to wear sealskin today because the endangered status of seals has been so well publicized.
12. It rained for a week, but we may be able to save the crop.
13. Most textbook authors are careful to define special terms.
14. The plant supervisor never gives one (or me or us workers) a chance to ask questions.
15. We argue constantly, and it bothers me that he never looks straight at me.

Chapter 13 Shifts

EXERCISE 1, p. 233

1. If a person has just moved to the city, he or she has trouble knowing where to go.
2. When taxpayers do not file on time, they have to pay a penalty.
3. Writers must know what they are writing about; otherwise they cannot write.
4. If a student misses too many classes, he or she may fail a course. Or: If students miss too many classes, they may fail a course. Or: If you miss too many classes, you may fail a course.
5. One should not judge other people's actions unless one knows the circumstances.

EXERCISE 2, p. 234

1. Soon after he joined the union, Lester <u>appeared</u> at a rally and <u>made</u> a speech.
2. First sand <u>down</u> any paint that is peeling; then <u>paint</u> the bare wood with primer.
3. Rachel is walking down the street, and suddenly she stops, as a shot <u>rings</u> out.
4. Rudeness occurs when people <u>do</u> not see themselves as others <u>see</u> them.
5. To buy a tape deck, find out what features you need and <u>decide</u> what you want to pay.

EXERCISE 3, p. 236

1. <u>They dug up</u> some arrowheads, and they found some pottery that was almost undamaged.
2. They started the game after <u>they ran</u> some practice drills.
3. The tornado ripped off the roof and <u>deposited it</u> in a nearby lot.
4. <u>The senator began</u> the debate when he introduced the new bill.
5. If you learn how to take good notes in class, you <u>will avoid</u> much extra work.

EXERCISE 4, p. 236

1. Coach Butler said that our timing was terrible and <u>that he would rather cancel the season than watch us play.</u> Or: Coach Butler said, "<u>Your timing is terrible.</u> I would rather cancel the season than watch you play."
2. The report concluded <u>that drought is a serious threat</u> and that we must begin conserving water now. Or: The report concluded, "Drought is a serious threat. <u>We must begin conserving water now.</u>"
3. Teachers who assign a lot of homework always say <u>that they are doing so for students' own good</u> and that they'd rather not hear any complaints. Or: Teachers who assign a lot of homework always say, "I'm doing this for your own good, <u>and I'd rather not hear any complaints.</u>"
4. The author claims that adults pass through emotional stages and <u>that no stage can be avoided.</u> Or: The author claims, "<u>Adults pass through emotional stages, and</u> no stage can be avoided."

5. My grandfather says <u>that gardening keeps him alive</u> and
    that, in any event, the exercise helps ease his arthritis.
    <u>Or:</u> My grandfather says, "Gardening helps keep me alive,
    <u>and,</u> in any event, the exercise helps ease <u>my</u> arthritis."

EXERCISE 5, p. 237

The shifts identified and labeled:

> <u>One</u> is always urged to conserve energy, and <u>we</u>
> [shift to first person] try to do that. However, saving
> energy requires making sacrifices. My children like
> baths, not showers, so how can I tell them <u>that they must</u>
> <u>keep clean</u> and then insist, "<u>You must not use the bath</u>"
> [shift to direct quotation]? They won't stay clean. <u>I</u>
> <u>don't mind</u> a cool house, but <u>it has to be kept warm</u>
> [shift to passive voice] when <u>you</u> [shift to second person]
> have the flu. <u>Everyone</u> [shift to third-person singular]
> <u>enjoys</u> a fire in the fireplace, but <u>they</u> [shift to third-
> person plural] <u>fail</u> to realize how much heat from the
> furnace <u>was</u> [shift to past tense] released up the chimney.
> Nonetheless, <u>we</u> [back to first person] <u>have to learn</u> to
> live with inconveniences or <u>be introduced</u> [shift to
> passive voice] to real hardship later on.

Possible revision:

> <u>We are</u> always urged to conserve energy, and we try
> to do that. However, saving energy requires making sacfi-
> fices. My children like baths, not showers, so how can I
> tell them that they must keep clean and then insist <u>that</u>
> <u>they must not use the bath</u>? They won't stay clean. I
> don't mind a cool house, but <u>I have to keep the house</u>
> warm when <u>someone</u> has the flu. Everyone enjoys a fire
> in the fireplace, but <u>no one realizes</u> how much heat from
> the furnace <u>is</u> released up the chimney. Nonetheless, we
> have to learn to live with inconveniences or <u>expect to</u>
> <u>meet</u> real hardship later on.

Chapter 14 <u>Misplaced and Dangling Modifiers</u>

EXERCISE 1, p. 240

1. <u>With a wink</u> the magician made a rabbit disappear.
2. The electric typewriter <u>on the desk</u> is running.
3. Marie opened the book <u>by Charles Dickens</u> given to her last Christmas.
4. We found the contact lens on the rug <u>during lunch</u>.
5. <u>In the kitchen</u> the little girl fed the kitten that she had received for Christmas.
6. The bell <u>that you hear chiming</u> is an heirloom.
7. The foundry delivered machines <u>in a truck</u> to the factory.
8. <u>With flashing eyes</u> she stared at the people standing nearby.
9. <u>From Niagara Falls</u>, Buffalo gains a huge supply of hydro-electric power that will never be exhausted.
10. <u>After the damage was done</u>, my father realized the mistakes he had made.

EXERCISE 2, p. 241

Sample answers:

1. a. <u>Almost</u> everybody hates him.
    b. Everybody <u>almost</u> hates him.
2. a. <u>Even</u> now I remember the details of the event.
    b. Now I remember <u>even</u> the details of the event.
3. a. We <u>hardly</u> heard him call our names.
    b. We heard him <u>hardly</u> call our names.
4. a. Write <u>simply</u>.
    b. <u>Simply</u> write.
5. a. Say <u>exactly</u> what you mean.
    b. Say what you mean <u>exactly</u>.

EXERCISE 3, p. 241

1. a. The baseball team that <u>most of the time</u> wins championships has excellent pitching.
    b. The baseball team that wins championships has excellent pitching <u>most of the time</u>.
2. a. <u>When the game was over</u>, I told my son I would play with him.
    b. I told my son I would play with him <u>when the game was over</u>.

3. a. A person who <u>often</u> skis gets cold.
    b. A person who skis gets cold <u>often</u>.
4. a. The man who was <u>totally</u> bald refused to seek a remedy.
    b. The man who was bald refused <u>totally</u> to seek a remedy.
5. a. People who <u>occasionally</u> see psychologists will feel better.
    b. People who see psychologists will <u>occasionally</u> feel better.

EXERCISE 4, p. 243

1. <u>Although he was later accused of dereliction of duty</u>, the lieutenant had given the correct orders.
2. The girls loved to sun <u>daily</u> beside the pool.
3. Ballet will be one of the country's most popular arts <u>if the present interest continues to grow</u>.
4. <u>After two days of silence</u>, the police revealed the story.
5. The beavers abandoned their dam <u>when the new housing construction began</u>.

EXERCISE 5, p. 245

Possible answers:

1. <u>While I was</u> staring at the ceiling, the idea became clear.
2. <u>Because his house was</u> sagging and needing a new coat of paint, Mr. Preston called the house painter.
3. By repairing the transmission, <u>we got</u> our car to run again.
4. <u>I let</u> Monday pass me by without <u>my</u> accomplishing anything.
5. To swim well, <u>one needs</u> good shoulder muscles.
6. To obtain disability income, <u>an employee must have a doctor certify that he or she cannot work</u>.
7. When <u>I was</u> only a ninth grader, my grandmother tried to teach me double-entry bookkeeping.
8. Arriving by train, <u>the traveler sees</u> the stockyards dominating the landscape.
9. After <u>he weighed</u> the alternatives, his decision became clear.
10. Although <u>the weather was</u> unusually hot, the rains kept the crops from being ruined.

EXERCISE 6, p. 246

Possible answers:

1. As we were taking our seats, the announcer read the line-up.
2. As I was rushing to the interview, my shoelace broke.
3. The children from the fifth grade crowded into the buses.
4. While trying to cheer Jason up, she terrified him instead with her Halloween mask.
5. They were holding hands when a man crept up behind them.
6. Wearing a yellow satin robe, she rested her bandaged foot on the stool.
7. At fifty years old, my uncle said he had never received good advice.
8. Several people who had been shopping in town saw the ranch hand.
9. When we reached the end of the road, a vast emptiness surrounded us.
10. The day after she returned from vacation, Sylvie received a letter announcing she had won.

Chapter 15   Mixed and Incomplete Sentences

EXERCISE 1, p. 250

Possible answers:

1. Because of a broken leg, Vance left the football team.
2. Schizophrenia is a psychological disorder causing a person to withdraw from reality and behave in abnormal ways.
3. The polished stones were all beyond my price range.
4. Any government that can support an expedition to Mars should be able to solve its country's social problems.
5. Different brewing methods produce the different tastes among beers.
6. Needlepoint is the craft of working with yarn on a mesh canvas.
7. The help of his staff got the mayor elected.
8. After mowing the backyard, we were ready for a glass of iced tea.
9. A divorce is the dissolution of a marriage contract by a judge.
10. Many people don't accept the theory of evolution because it contradicts their religious beliefs.

EXERCISE 2, p. 254

1. Both of them not only believe <u>in</u> but work for energy con-
    servation.
2. The legal question raised by the prosecution was relevant
    and <u>was</u> considered by the judge.
3. Foot<u>ball</u> interested Ralph more than his friends <u>did</u>. <u>Or:</u>
    Football interested Ralph more than <u>it did</u> his friends.
4. His tip was larger than <u>that of</u> any <u>other</u> customer I ever
    waited on.
5. With an altitude of 6288 feet, Mount Washington is higher
    than any <u>other</u> mountain in New Hampshire.
6. The largest bookstore <u>in</u> the United States stocks two <u>or</u>
    three copies <u>of</u> most books in print.
7. My dog is only a puppy; the cats <u>are</u> both ten years old.
8. My chemistry text is more interesting to me than <u>any</u>
    social science text.
9. He feared <u>that</u> darkness and the drop in temperature would
    trap the climbers on the mountain.
10. Inventors usually have an interest <u>in</u> and <u>a</u> talent for
    solving practical problems.

Part IV

EFFECTIVE SENTENCES

Chapter 16 Using Coordination and Subordination

EXERCISE 1, p. 259

Possible revisions:

1. Everyone read fairy tales as a child, and everyone remem-
   bers some. Most people think they are only for children,
   for they express the deepest fears and desires of children; but they also express the deepest fears and desires
   of adults. Adults read them to children, yet they should
   read them for themselves.
2. Henry Hudson was an English explorer, but he captained
   ships for the Dutch East India Company. On a voyage in
   1610 he passed by Greenland and sailed into a great bay
   in today's northern Canada. He thought he and his
   sailors could winter there, but the cold was terrible
   and food ran out. The sailors mutinied and cast Hudson
   and eight others adrift in a small boat. Hudson and his
   companions perished.

EXERCISE 2, p. 259

Possible answers:

1. Although the dean let the police know she was furious,
   they refused to listen and began patrolling the campus.
2. The Chinese are communists, which means that they believe
   in the common ownership of goods and the means to produce
   them.
3. Wanting freedom, the dogs escaped from the pen when the
   keeper forgot to secure the latch. They ran away, and it
   took us the rest of the day to find them.
4. Although the weather in March is cold and rainy, sometimes
   it is warm and sunny. Everyone wants to be outdoors after
   the long winter, but the inconsistency in weather makes it
   impossible to plan outdoor activities.

5. I froze when the gun sounded, but an instant later I was running with a smooth, pumping motion. I knew I would win the race.
6. Because they are determined to preserve their environment, the citizens of Vermont have some of the nation's toughest antipollution laws.
7. Although two days last month were legal holidays, the school held classes as usual.
8. Registering for classes the first time is confusing because you have to find your way around and deal with strangers.
9. Robert was due to arrive at lunchtime but didn't, and he didn't call until just before dinner.
10. Although air traffic in and out of major cities increases yearly so that congestion is becoming dangerous, the current regulations are inadequate to control even the present traffic.

EXERCISE 3, p. 264

1. a. In World War I, German forces set out to capture Verdun, which was a fortress in northeastern France.
   b. In World War I, German forces set out to capture Verdun, a fortress in northeastern France.
2. a. One of the largest salt mines in the world, lying under a city in Poland, yields an average of 60,000 tons of salt yearly.
   b. Yielding an average of 60,000 tons of salt yearly, one of the largest salt mines in the world lies under a city in Poland.
3. a. Bertrand Russell was raised by his grandparents because he had been orphaned in early childhood.
   b. Bertrand Russell, orphaned in early childhood, was raised by his grandparents.
4. a. James Joyce, who has been praised as the greatest writer since Milton and condemned as a writer of "latrine literature," is one of the century's most controversial writers.
   b. Praised as the greatest writer since Milton and condemned as a writer of "latrine literature," James Joyce is one of the century's most controversial writers.
5. a. The Amish live peaceful but austere lives, most of them refusing to use modern technology.
   b. Living peaceful but austere lives, most of the Amish refuse to use modern technology.

6. a. Hernando de Soto, who is the legendary European dis-
        coverer of the Mississippi River, supposedly died on the
        river's banks.
    b. Hernando de Soto, the legendary European discoverer
        of the Mississippi River, supposedly died on the river's
        banks.
7. a. Because computerized newspaper operations speed up
        and simplify copy preparation, they are favored by edi-
        tors and reporters.
    b. Favored by editors and reporters, computerized news-
        paper operations speed up and simplify copy preparation.
8. a. Although patents are the surest protection for inven-
        tions, they are difficult to obtain.
    b. Patents, the surest protection for inventions, are
        difficult to obtain.
9. a. Speaking at Westminster College in Missouri, Winston
        Churchill originated the phrase "the Iron Curtain."
    b. Winston Churchill originated the phrase "the Iron
        Curtain" at Westminster College in Missouri.
10. a. Andrew Bradford, who first published <u>American Maga-
        zine</u> in 1741, began the American magazine industry.
    b. When Andrew Bradford first published <u>American Maga-
        zine</u> in 1741, he began the American magazine industry.

EXERCISE 4, p. 265

Possible revision:

    Many students today are no longer majoring in the
liberal arts--<u>that is, in</u> such subjects as history,
English, and the social sciences. <u>Although</u> students
think a liberal arts degree will not help them get jobs,
they are wrong. They may not get practical, job-related
experience from the liberal arts, but they will get a
broad education <u>that will</u> never again be available to
them. Many employers look for more than a technical,
professional education <u>because</u> they think such an education can make an employee's views too narrow. <u>Instead,
they</u> want open-minded employees <u>who can</u> think about
problems from many angles. <u>This sort of flexibility--
vital to the health of our society--is just what the
liberal arts curriculum instills.</u>

EXERCISE 5, p. 265

Possible answers:

1. My boss's new car, parked in front of the store, rolled into my bike.
2. Basketball is a game of surprises, with the best plays sometimes being made at the last minute.
3. Because reasonable people no longer think that there's anything wrong with women who want to become career officers, a woman who wants a career in the armed forces is better off now.
4. Children should understand that the truly entertaining television shows are those that take some thought to enjoy.
5. Though invited on short notice when our planned speaker canceled, the Sierra Club speaker nonetheless gave an informative and moving talk about our need to preserve wilderness areas from extinction.

EXERCISE 6, p. 268

1. Because I was going home for Thanksgiving, my mother cooked a squash pie for me.
2. From where I was sitting, the car looked as if it would hit the baby carriage.
3. Busing schoolchildren is a major issue in many cities, but in others it does not seem to arouse much interest.
4. Because teachers and legislators worry about the literacy of high school students, the situation may improve.
5. Many states give minimum competency tests for graduation from high school, as if there weren't enough hurdles to jump over to get a high school diploma.

EXERCISE 7, p. 268

Possible revision:

   Although many people claim that chemical fertilizers and insecticides are essential for a healthy and productive vegetable garden, they are wrong. Organic-gardening methods produce healthy gardens. Good, nutritious soil will give any plant a head start on healthy growth. The most necessary soil element is nitrogen, supplied by

several organic sources <u>including</u> animal manure and fish-
meal. Aerated soil allows roots room to grow <u>and</u> water
to drain easily. <u>Since</u> pests like mites and beetles have
their place in the <u>food chain, using</u> insecticides to kill
them can result in larger populations of <u>other, more</u>
<u>troublesome pests that they feed on.</u> A strong plant in
good soil will resist attack from pests. A gardener can
also <u>discourage pests with</u> exotic concoctions of strong-
smelling ingredients like beer, onions, and red <u>peppers,</u>
<u>for</u> pests react much as we do to the strong odors. And
practiced gardeners know <u>how to discourage pests</u> by
growing certain plants next to others. For example,
green beans will <u>keep beetles away from eggplants, and</u>
leeks will keep flies away from carrots.

Chapter 17 <u>Using Parallelism</u>

EXERCISE 1, p. 272

1. Three parallel participles--<u>whining</u>, <u>blowing</u>, <u>drying</u>--
    modify the appositive <u>wind</u>. Two parallel proper nouns
    --<u>Cajon</u>, <u>San Gorgonio</u>--accompany <u>Passes</u>, and <u>drying</u> has
    two parallel objects, <u>the hills and the nerves</u>. The
    series of three participial phrases sweeps the sentence
    along in imitation of the wind it is describing.
2. The two phrases are exactly parallel, with two compara-
    tive adjectives modifying two nouns. The structure is
    perfect for a sentence stating a relationship between two
    objects.
3. The three subject complements--<u>gray</u>, <u>deadened</u>, and <u>wintry</u>
    --are paralleled by the three adjectives modifying <u>cold-</u>
    <u>ness</u>--<u>slow</u>, <u>moist</u>, and <u>heavy</u>. Also parallel are the two
    gerunds, <u>sinking</u> and <u>deadening</u>. The parallelism empha-
    sizes the heavy bleakness of the day.
4. Supporting <u>pleasantest</u> is a wealth of detail expressed in
    five parallel absolute phrases: <u>exhaustion . . . in</u>; <u>the</u>
    <u>sated mosquitoes . . . off</u>; <u>the room . . . garments</u>; <u>the</u>
    <u>vines . . . day</u>; and <u>the air conditioner . . . mosquitoes</u>.
    The phrases convey no action, emphasizing the stillness
    of the scene.
5. The limiting effects of aging are emphasized by the in-
    creasingly narrow parallel verbs--<u>paints</u>, <u>lies</u>, <u>imprisons</u>--
    and the parallel objects--<u>every action</u>, <u>every movement</u>,
    and <u>every thought</u>.

EXERCISE 2, p. 272

Possible answers:

1. For exercise I prefer swimming and <u>jogging</u>.
2. After a week on a construction job, Leon felt not so much exhausted as <u>invigorated</u> by the physical labor.
3. To lose weight, cut down on the amount you eat, eat fewer calories in the food you do consume, and <u>exercise</u> regularly.
4. All persons are entitled <u>both to equal</u> educational opportunities and <u>to equal</u> employment opportunities.
5. Everyone was surprised at the election results: overwhelming approval of the bond issue; <u>defeat of</u> the redistricting plan; and <u>all new faces on</u> the city council.
6. My father insisted that I learn how to budget and <u>how to create and manage</u> a bank account.
7. Her generosity, <u>sympathy</u>, and <u>ability to</u> motivate employees make her an excellent supervisor.
8. Pam hoped for either a loan or <u>a part-time job</u>.
9. Baby-sitting children, I have learned how to <u>be amusing, patient, and both</u> stern and fair.
10. The shock of having one's apartment burglarized comes less from <u>missing</u> possessions than <u>from thinking</u> of a stranger <u>invading</u> one's privacy.

EXERCISE 3, p. 274

Possible answers:

1. The class is held on Wednesday afternoons and sometimes on Saturday mornings.
2. Dick finally held on to a job after lasting three weeks at his previous job, two weeks at an earlier job, and three days at the job before that.
3. After making several costly mistakes, he stopped to consider the jobs available to him and his goals for a job.
4. To make a good stew, marinate the meat, add plenty of vegetables, include wine for flavor, and simmer the whole thing for at least two hours.
5. Carlone had three desires: first, money; second, fame; and third, happiness.
6. Driving a car with a manual transmission requires mastering the gears, coordinating the clutch and gas pedals, and attending to the sounds of the engine.
7. The sun looks small at its zenith but large at the horizon.

8. Ben walked with a limp and a bent back.
9. Most people who saw the movie were unimpressed with or
    frankly critical of the acting.
10. We returned from camping tired, dirty, and covered with
    mosquito bites.

Chapter 18   Emphasizing Main Ideas

EXERCISE 1, p. 280

1. The main clause is One . . . Mouse.   The sentence is
    cumulative.   Rewritten as a periodic sentence:

    An idiot optimist, each week marching forth in Techni-
    color against a battalion of cats, invariably humiliating
    them with one clever trick after another, Walt Disney's
    Mickey Mouse was one of the most disastrous cultural in-
    fluences ever to hit America.

2. The main clause is I . . . house.   The sentence is
    periodic.   Rewritten as a cumulative sentence:

    I set up the frame of my house at length, in the beginning
    of May, with the help of some of my acquaintances, rather
    to improve so good an occasion for neighborliness than
    from any necessity.

3. The main clause is the . . . Washington.   The sentence is
    periodic.   Rewritten as a cumulative sentence:

    The farmers marched on Washington because they wanted a
    fair price for their crops and felt the government was
    not doing enough for them.

4. The main clause is Matthew's . . . jail.   The sentence is
    cumulative.   Rewritten as a periodic sentence:

    Writing letters, seeing lawyers, and attending meetings--
    because they knew their father to be honest and believed
    him to be innocent--Matthew's children worked two years
    to get him out of jail.

5. The main clause is <u>The . . . flight</u>. The sentence is periodic. Rewritten as a cumulative sentence:

The swan took flight, its neck stretched forward, its wings beating against the water.

EXERCISE 2, p. 280

Possible answers:

1. Cumulative: The combined technology of computers and television will dramatically change our lives in the few years remaining before the end of the century.
Periodic: In the few years remaining before the end of the century, the combined technology of computers and television will dramatically change our lives.
2. Cumulative: The abandoned car was a neighborhood eyesore, its windows smashed, its body rusted and dented.
Periodic: Its windows smashed, its body rusted and dented, the abandoned car was a neighborhood eyesore.
3. Cumulative: Two trains raced across the river, their wheels spinning, their engines parallel and billowing smoke.
Periodic: Their wheels spinning, their engines parallel and billowing smoke, two trains raced across the river.
4. Cumulative: Carl hid his shame, walking with his back straight, holding his head high, and staring straight ahead.
Periodic: Walking with his back straight, holding his head high, and staring straight ahead, Carl hid his shame.
5. Cumulative: The leaf fell slowly, wafted by the wind and performing graceful somersaults.
Periodic: Wafted by the wind and performing graceful somersaults, the leaf fell slowly.

EXERCISE 3, p. 281

1. The explosion at the chemical factory started a fire in a building, blew up half a city block, and killed six workers.
2. In the 1950s Americans wanted to keep up with the Joneses; in the 1980s Americans want to keep up with change.
3. People view heaven in several ways: as a myth, as just another world, as the promise of future happiness, or as the presence of God.

4. When Claire thought of her husband, she shivered; but
   when she thought of her old friend Carl, she smiled.
5. The football players marched triumphantly into the locker
   room, battered, bruised, and victorious.

EXERCISE 4, p. 283

Possible answers:

1. Without rain our seeds will not germinate; <u>without rain
   we will have no crops</u>.
2. Roger worked harder than usual to win the chemistry prize
   that his father had won before him. <u>He could not let his
   father down</u>.
3. My parents fear <u>change in</u> morals, <u>change in</u> their neighborhood, and <u>change in</u> their own children.
4. By the time the rescuers reached the crash site, the wind
   had nearly covered the small plane with snow. <u>No one had
   survived</u>.
5. The key to staying happy is staying free: <u>free of</u> debt,
   <u>free of</u> possessions, and <u>free of</u> entangling relationships.

EXERCISE 5, p. 285

Possible answers:

1. <u>The government told</u> the residents to evacuate their
   homes when <u>it</u> discovered dangerous amounts of contaminants
   in their water.
2. <u>We must be able</u> to get out of this predicament, whether
   legally or illegally.
3. The <u>problem is</u> that we owe more taxes than we can afford.
4. <u>Art dealers looked over</u> the paintings before the auction
   began.
5. After all these years <u>no good road runs</u> between Spring-
   field and Lyndon.

EXERCISE 6, p. 285

Possible revision:

   The most famous fairy tale, "Cinderella," is also
the most popular. Badly treated by her stepmother and
stepsisters, who make her do all the chores, Cinderella

finally finds rescue in her fairy godmother and marries
a handsome prince. The climactic episode--when the
prince can fit the glass slipper only on Cinderella's
tiny, delicate foot--shows the tale's origin in ninth-
century China, where small feet were a mark of special
beauty for women. We may now be less fascinated with
small feet, but we are still fascinated with Cinderella's
story. In Europe and the United States alone, the tale
exists today in over 500 versions.

Chapter 19   Achieving Variety

EXERCISE 1, p. 289

Possible revisions:

1.   Any supermarket shopper has seen the Red Devil on
    small cans of meat spreads like deviled ham. The trade-
    mark of Underwood, the Red Devil is the oldest registered
    trademark in the United States. A ·trademark identifies
    a product by linking it clearly to a particular maker.
    Although an original trademark can become legally estab-
    lished with continued use, registration with the U.S.
    Patent Office can provide further protection. Infringe-
    ments of trademarks are punishable by law.

2.   Nathaniel Hawthorne was one of America's first great
    writers. He was descended from a judge who had presided
    at some of the Salem witch trials and had condemned some
    men and women to death. Hawthorne could never forget
    about this piece of family history, and he always felt
    guilty about it. Though he never wrote about his ancestor
    directly, he did write about the darkness of the human
    heart. In The Scarlet Letter and The House of the Seven
    Gables, he demonstrated his favorite theme: a secret sin.

EXERCISE 2, p. 291

1. Voting rights for women seemed a possibility in the 1860s.
   Yet women were not actually given the vote for nearly
   sixty years.

2. Although Robert had orders to stay in bed, he returned to
   work immediately.

3. Gasoline prices are determined by international conditions we cannot control. <u>Therefore</u>, they may never stabilize.
4. <u>Carefully handling the ropes</u>, the rescuers lowered the frightened climber from the ledge.
5. <u>If</u> the building is torn down, we will all be without homes.

EXERCISE 3, p. 292

   <u>When Fred found himself cut off from the rest of the campers</u>, he sat down to try to get his bearings. <u>Carefully watching the movement of the sun</u>, he thought he would find his way before nightfall. <u>But</u> he was still lost when the stars came out. <u>Finally</u>, he admitted he was lost and covered himself in leaves for warmth.

EXERCISE 4, p. 294

Sample answers:

1. How many cars are registered on this campus?
2. Try to find a parking space on this campus any weekday morning after nine o'clock.
3. What an unexpected pleasure it was to find a parking space within two blocks of the library!
4.   Can the frustration caused by the parking problem be healthy for the student? He drives round and round the campus, the minutes of lost study or class time ticking away. Tension builds. As he passes filled row upon filled row in one lot after another, the driver begins to tremble, sweat, and swear. And the anger and panic, instead of abating when finally the car is safely stowed, stay with the student throughout the day.

EXERCISE 5, p. 294

1. The shortest sentence (1) is one word; the longest (4) is thirty-two words. A cumulative sentence, this longest one draws out the learned value of love and emphasizes the repeated subject of the adverb clause (<u>nothing . . . nothing . . . nothing</u>) by lengthening it each time. In contrast, the periodic construction implied by the last sentence (though its form is compound, it means <u>If I say I hate you . . .</u>) makes the sentence sound conclusive,

deliberate. Also deliberate is the next-to-last sentence
in which both independent clauses begin with expletives
and contain modifying subordinate clauses. The two parts
of the paragraph and its two topics are marked particularly by the shift from the passive verbs used for love
(which we are taught) to the active verbs used for hate
(which we learn by ourselves).

2. Again, the shortest sentence is one word: <u>No</u>. The
   longest is sentence 5, <u>I pictured the man as</u>. . . . The
   opening periodic sentence sets the scene before coming to
   the point. The longest sentence gains its length and
   power from the six modifying verbal phrases that convey
   Wright's first impression of Mencken. Wright relies on
   questions interspersed with tentative answers to show his
   own incremental awakening on discovering Mencken. Repe-
   tition--<u>fighting</u>, <u>fighting</u>; <u>using</u> . . . <u>using</u>; <u>maybe</u>,
   <u>perhaps</u>--also shows Wright wrestling with what he has
   found. The last question leads to the conclusion of the
   final three sentences, which gradually increase in length
   and complexity.

Part V

PUNCTUATION

Chapter 20   End Punctuation

EXERCISE 1, p. 297

1. Let the dissenters have their say.
2. The police asked whose dog was barking.
3. Class begins at 3:00 P.M. sharp.
4. The new house had 2200 sq. ft. of heated space.
5. The Roman Empire in the West collapsed in 476 A.D.

EXERCISE 2, p. 298

1. Parents often wonder whether their children are getting anything out of college.
2. "What does ontogeny mean?" the biology instructor asked.
3. The candidate for Congress asked whether there was anything he could do to help us.
4. Will little children always ask, "Well, if God made everything, who made God?"
5. Ulysses and his mariners took seven years to travel from Troy to Ithaca. Or was it six? Or eight?

EXERCISE 3, p. 300

1. The sun was so bright that it bleached all colors.
2. "Well, now!" he said loudly.
3. The child's cries could be heard next door: "Don't go! Don't go!"
4. Punctuation correct.
5. As the fire fighters moved their equipment into place, police walked through the crowd shouting, "Move back!"

EXERCISE 4, p. 300

When Maureen approached Jesse with her idea for a
class gift to the school, he asked if she knew how much
it would cost. "Forget it if it's over $200," he said.
"Do you think the class can come up with even that much?"
Both of them knew the committee treasury contained only
the $100 given by Dr. Wheeler. Maureen said she thought
they could raise the rest with a talent show. "That's
ridiculous!" exclaimed Jesse. "What talent? Yours? Dr.
Wheeler's? Whose?" But he softened when Maureen asked
him if he would perform his animal imitations. Jesse
loved to do animal imitations.

Chapter 21   The Comma

EXERCISE 1, p. 302

1. Kampala is Uganda's capital and largest city, and it
    serves as the nation's social and economic center.
2. I am looking for a job, but the ones I find either pay
    too little or require too many skills that I do not have.
3. Housing prices continue to rise, so fewer people can
    afford their own homes.
4. Jill wanted to go out for the tennis team, but she
    strained a tendon in her right ankle.
5. The hikers had come a long way, and they could not summon
    the energy for the final mile to the river and a comfort-
    able campsite.

EXERCISE 2, p. 303

1. The accident must have happened at night, or it could not
    have happened at all.
2. The FBI used to be considered simply a crime-busting
    organization, but now we know it is involved in national
    security as well.
3. His father sometimes hit him, so the boy sometimes hit
    his little sister.
4. In many bird species the female builds the nest, and the
    male defends it.
5. The last Super Bowl game was a bore, yet we all watched
    it from beginning to end.

EXERCISE 3, p. 304

1. Gasping for breath, the fire fighters staggered out of the burning building.
2. Because of the late morning rain, the baseball game had to be canceled.
3. Correct without comma.
4. Without so much as nodding her head, Phyllis slammed the door and left.
5. Before you make any more mistakes, read the directions.
6. Correct without comma.
7. Even though Regina was sick last week, she attended every rehearsal.
8. Correct without comma.
9. When young, Robert was tall for his age.
10. In both the North and the South, schools are more integrated now than they were fifteen years ago.

EXERCISE 4, p. 305

1. To vote wisely, one needs objective information about the candidates' backgrounds and opinions.
2. If the city goes deeper into debt, services will have to be curtailed.
3. Snapping in the wind, the flags made the speaker's message seem even more urgent.
4. With only 108 acres, Vatican City is the smallest sovereign state in the world.
5. Although a woman was finally appointed as a Supreme Court justice, the Court remains far from balanced.

EXERCISE 5, p. 310

1. Moby Dick, a novel by Herman Melville, is thought by some critics to be America's finest novel.
2. Our modern ideas about civil liberties can be traced back to the Magna Carta, which was written in 1215.
3. Legionnaire's disease, unknown until a few years ago, has been responsible for the deaths of many people.
4. The poem is by the fiction writer Jay Berde.
5. Please listen, fellow voters, while I explain my position.
6. Correct without commas.
7. All students working to support themselves should be given some financial aid.

8. The port of New York, which was once the busiest in the
    nation, is not nearly as active as it was.
9. Correct without commas.
10. Those of us who hadn't seen the concert felt we had
    missed something.

EXERCISE 6, p. 311

Possible answers:

1. The calculator, which has limited use, is the size of a
    quarter.
2. Joan Silver, leading the runners, was the first to come
    in view.
3. A house on Langness Street is over two hundred years old.
4. Men and women who control our industries are interested
    primarily in profits.
5. The senator, William de Silva, is a native of this city.
6. Winter, the best of seasons, is a time of dazzling snows
    and toasty fires.
7. The island, in the middle of the river, is a perfect
    hideaway.
8. The demonstrators blocking the road tied up traffic for
    two hours.
9. Psychologists say that children, who have difficulty
    evaluating their own performances, need the constant sup-
    port of their parents.
10. Courses that sharpen communications skills should be re-
    quired of medical and nursing students.

EXERCISE 7, p. 312

1. The shooting having started, the set was quiet except for
    the actors' voices.
2. Their exams finished, the students had a party to cele-
    brate.
3. The painters quit work early, the house painted and the
    supplies put away.
4. The police drove away from the accident, their investiga-
    tion completed.
5. Spring coming nearer, the ground felt damp and the air
    smelled fresh.
6. The governor had a chance, the legislature being in
    recess, to enhance his position with the voters.
7. All doors secured, the guard took a nap.

8. The case was finally closed, the only suspect having died.
9. Children, their imaginations being vivid, often suffer from terrifying nightmares.
10. The exam being difficult, he was lucky to pass the course.

EXERCISE 8, p. 313

1. The president should have a single term of six years, not two four-year terms.
2. The humidity, not just the heat, makes some summer days unbearable.
3. It was William Faulkner, not F. Scott Fitzgerald, who won the Nobel Prize.
4. World War II ended with the surrender of the Japanese in September 1945, not with the surrender of the Germans in May.
5. My family attends church in Cromwell, not Durben, because we know the minister in Cromwell.

EXERCISE 9, p. 315

1. For his second birthday I'd like to buy my son a plastic hammer, a punching bag, and a leash.
2. Neither personal loss, business setbacks, nor illness defeated him.
3. Correct without comma.
4. That morning, fresh, crisp, and clear, turned out to be memorable.
5. Television newscasters rarely work full-time as reporters, investigate only light stories if any, and rarely write the copy they read on the air.
6. Correct without comma.
7. Several stores opened new, larger branches in the shopping mall outside the city.
8. The suspect was brought in kicking, hitting, and cursing.
9. She was a Miamian by birth, a farmer by temperament, and a worker to the day she died.
10. The unset leg fracture she had as a child caused her troubling, annoying pain all her life.

EXERCISE 10, p. 317

1. The world's population exceeds 4,415,000,000.

2. Boulder, Colorado, sits at the base of the Rocky Mountains.
3. The letter was postmarked October 2, 1981, in Paris, France.
4. Whoever writes P.O. Box 725, Asheville, North Carolina 28803, will get a quick response.
5. January 1, 2000, will be a big day in our lives.

EXERCISE 11, p. 319

1. "The mass of men lead lives of quiet desperation," Henry David Thoreau wrote in Walden.
2. "I'll be on the next bus for Cleveland," the woman promised.
3. In a sentence that has stirred generations of readers, Jean-Jacques Rousseau announced, "Man was born free, and everywhere he is in chains."
4. "We must face reality," the president said sternly, "while we have time."
5. "The team has a chance," the announcer said quietly. Then he yelled, "We have a chance!"

EXERCISE 12, p. 320

1. Beginning tomorrow, afternoon practice will be canceled. Or: Beginning tomorrow afternoon, practice will be canceled.
2. Though old, Grandfather was still spry.
3. However crude, the invention is promising.
4. Of the fifty, six boys can't go.
5. Those who can't, regret it.

EXERCISE 13, p. 323

1. Classes had to be held in the hallways because of the fire damage.
2. Charles Dickens's novel David Copperfield is still a favorite of generations of readers.
3. The split season after the baseball strike in 1981 gave more teams a chance to win the pennant.
4. The coach said that next year the team would have a winning season.
5. Sentence correct as punctuated.
6. The tennis term love, meaning "zero," comes from the French word l'oeuf, meaning "the egg."

7. The complicated gears on a ten-speed bicycle_make it difficult to maintain and repair.
8. Cheese, eggs, and milk_are high in cholesterol.
9. Mary bought some of her course books at a used-book store_ and borrowed the rest.
10. Sentence correct as punctuated.
11. After the New Hampshire primary_eliminates some candidates, the presidential race calms down somewhat.
12. The cat brought home a dirty, smelly_sock.
13. The point_of many of F. Scott Fitzgerald's stories_is that having money does not guarantee happiness.
14. Forest fires often benefit_the woods they burn.
15. Guidebooks single out the bird sanctuary north of town_ and the marsh south of town.

EXERCISE 14, p. 324

Ellis Island, New York, has reopened for business, but now the customers are tourists, not immigrants. This spot, which lies in New York Harbor, was the first American soil seen_or touched by many of the nation's immigrants. Though other places also served as ports of entry for foreigners, none has the symbolic power of_ Ellis Island. Between its opening in 1892 and its closing in 1954, over 20 million people, about two-thirds of all immigrants, were detained there before taking up their new lives in the United States. Ellis Island processed over 2000 (or 2,000) newcomers a day when immigration was at its peak between 1900 and 1920.

As the end of a long voyage and the introduction to the New World, Ellis Island must have left something to be desired. The "huddled masses," as the Statue of Liberty calls them, indeed were huddled. New arrivals were herded about, kept standing in lines for hours or days, yelled at, and abused. Assigned numbers, they submitted their bodies to the pokings and proddings of the silent nurses and doctors_who were charged with ferreting out the slightest sign_of sickness, disability, or insanity. That test having been passed, the immigrants faced interrogation by an official through an interpreter. Those_with names deemed inconveniently long or difficult to pronounce_often found themselves permanently labeled with abbreviations_of their names_or with the names_of their hometowns. But, of course, millions survived the examination, humiliation, and confusion_to take the last, short boat ride to New York City.

For many of them and especially for their descendants,
Ellis Island eventually became, not a nightmare, but the
place where life began.

Chapter 22   The Semicolon

EXERCISE 1, p. 325

1. Karate is not just a technique for self-defense; like a
   religion, it teaches inner calm.
2. He is still playing baseball at the age of sixty-three;
   he is still no good.
3. The Himalayas are the loftiest mountain range in the
   world; they culminate in the highest mountain in the
   world, Mount Everest.
4. Subways in New York City are noisy, dirty, and dangerous;
   they are also a superbly efficient means of transportation.
5. The pony express was slow but competent; the Postal
   Service is just slow.

EXERCISE 2, p. 326

Possible answers:

1. They said they were willing to work for little pay; the
   summer had been boring so far.
2. She drove a good car and wore expensive clothes; she
   relied on these external symbols to gain her popularity.
3. Indian rugs are deceptively decorative; their designs and
   colors have religious meanings for the weavers.
4. The storm blew down all the trees but the poplars; they
   stood in a row, undamaged.
5. The legend that Betsy Ross designed the first American
   flag is probably untrue; historians have never found any
   evidence to support it.

EXERCISE 3, p. 327

1. Thanksgiving was fewer than three weeks away; still, they
   had made no plans for the big turkey dinner.

2. Environmentalists are trying to preserve the meadow outside town; moreover, they sued some land developers who
   were planning to build in the city park.
3. The elevator shakes when it goes down; the inspector says
   it is safe, however.
4. We must cut down on our fuel consumption; otherwise,
   we'll find ourselves with no fuel, not just less.
5. The air was suddenly calm; consequently, we had to paddle
   our sailboat to shore.

EXERCISE 4, p. 328

Possible answers:

1. They didn't enjoy their first swim in the ocean because
   they were afraid of the waves; besides, the salty water
   was unpleasant.
2. He was alarmed by the shadow that stood suddenly in his
   path; nonetheless, he kept walking.
3. My grandfather grew up in Italy but never spoke Italian
   in the United States; instead, he always spoke English.
4. Peanuts thrive in light, sandy soil; thus, they are an
   ideal crop for the South, where such soil is common.
5. The speaker's nervousness showed in his damp brow and
   trembling voice; moreover, his hands shook so badly that
   he could barely hold his notes.

EXERCISE 5, p. 329

1. By evening, having looked at every house on the realtor's
   list, the Morianis were exhausted and crabby; but they
   still hadn't found anything they could afford to buy.
2. James did whatever he wanted, without regard for the
   feelings or welfare of those around him or for the harm
   he was doing to himself; and eventually he got into
   trouble.
3. Seeking lower taxes, businesses moved to the suburbs, and
   merchants closed their downtown stores in favor of new
   ones in the shopping mall; and the city's center died.
4. She had a challenging job, a decent income, and good
   prospects for the future; but she remained miserable.
5. The inside of the dorm has to be cleaned, painted, and
   furnished by September; or two hundred students will have
   no place to live.

EXERCISE 6, p. 329

Possible answers:

1. Scientists do not have the means to count the stars, planets, and moons in the universe; so they must rely on estimates.

2. Transportation is scarce and expensive in Alaska because of the extremely cold climate and sparse population; and the difficulties of transportation discourage businesses from locating there.

3. Legends of the towns of the Old West create a lively picture of constant saloon brawls, bank robberies, and gunfights; but the picture is inaccurate.

4. Most Americans believe that the Internal Revenue Service reads their tax returns carefully, checking and double-checking all the information they provide; and the IRS counts on this belief to keep taxpayers honest.

5. In the office Mrs. Brown was a tyrant who expected her subordinates to do exactly as she said; yet at home she was a pushover who let her children do whatever they pleased.

EXERCISE 7, p. 330

1. The picnic was a disaster from the start because Brian forgot the beach blankets and chairs; Julie forgot the beer, potato salad, and hot dogs; and Sam forgot his bathing suit.

2. The convocation droned on and on, with the college president intoning the challenges of education; the dean, first thanking the president, detailing the joys of education; and the student government president, thanking both the president and the dean, listing students' responsibilities to the college.

3. We have a cat who is the size of a cocker spaniel, with a bark to match; a dog who is so big we can't trust him in the house; and neighbors who, for some reason, won't speak to us.

4. The car, with its headlights out, swerved into oncoming traffic; narrowly missed a large, loaded oil truck; and headed, nose first, into a deep, muddy ditch.

5. The farm we visited has a clear, fast-moving brook; a shallow but clear pond; and trees, hundreds of trees that keep the waters and the house delightfully cool.

EXERCISE 8, p. 331

Possible answers:

1. Driving west from Pennsylvania, we saw vast expanses of tall corn and shorter soybean plants; many cows, some horses, and a few sheep grazing in rolling pastures; and sturdy, well-kept houses with matching barns.
2. The campaign took an unexpected turn when the Republican had to undergo an operation that kept her in the hospital for two weeks; the Democrat's wife gave birth to twins, a boy and a girl; and an independent candidate accused the other two of graft.
3. California's Fresno County, the nation's leading county in farm production, produces vegetables such as potatoes and tomatoes; fruits such as figs, peaches, and nectarines; and field and seed crops like alfalfa, barley, and cotton.
4. When the new building opened, visitors reacted to it with praise for the architect's choice of materials, sense of style, and imagination; with criticism of the building's excessive use of glass and too-sharp corners; and with boredom at the sight of yet another high-rise office tower.
5. With attention and practice we Americans should have no trouble learning the essential metric weights and measures, including the meter, about 39 inches; the kilogram, about 2.2 pounds; and the liter, about 1.06 quarts.

EXERCISE 9, p. 333

1. Thinking of her future, Marie decided to major in economics.
2. The bus line finally went out of business because more and more students drove themselves to school.
3. Even though the National League usually wins the All-Star Game, I think the American League is superior.
4. Despite our grasping for material goods, only three things are necessary for survival: sound shelter, warm clothes, and simple food.
5. Walking is great fun; we don't do enough of it. You see things when you're walking that you don't see when you're driving. You can smell and feel different things, too. Walking makes you a part of life. Driving just races you through it.

EXERCISE 10, p. 334

The movie's set, sounds, and actors captured the
essence of horror films. The set was ideal: dark,
deserted streets; trees dipping their branches over the
sidewalks; mist hugging the ground and creeping up to
meet the trees; looming shadows of unlighted, turreted
houses. The sounds, too, were appropriate; especially
terrifying was the hard, hollow sound of footsteps
echoing throughout the film. But the movie's best
feature was its actors, all of them tall, pale, and thin
to the point of emaciation. With one exception, they
were dressed uniformly in gray and had gray hair. The
exception was an actress who dressed only in black, as
if to set off her pale yellow, nearly white, long hair,
the only color in the film. The glinting black eyes of
another actor stole almost every scene; indeed, they
were the source of all the film's mischief.

Chapter 23   The Apostrophe

EXERCISE 1, p. 336

1. The mayor's announcement was expected.
2. Higher pay and three weeks' vacation were the focus of the
   garbage collectors' strike.
3. John Adams's letters to his wife illuminate his character.
4. Her sister-in-law's family was wealthy.
5. Everyone's books were stolen from the gym.
6. The Reagans' life-style was often criticized.
7. Children's clothes are ridiculously expensive.
8. Marvin and Colleen's child has a learning disability.
9. Susan's and Sarah's husbands are both out of work.
10. The utility companies' recent price increases are unlaw-
    ful.
11. We studied Keats's poetry.
12. An hour's reading was the only assignment.
13. Charles's new car was a lemon.
14. The Hickses' decision to move upset their children.
15. For goodness' sake, don't holler.

EXERCISE 2, p. 337

1. The neatest room was <u>hers</u>.
2. Punctuation correct.
3. The <u>Whites'</u> yard made <u>ours</u> look good.
4. Punctuation correct.
5. <u>Books</u> can be good <u>friends</u>.
6. Punctuation correct.
7. Punctuation correct.
8. Street crime was a particular focus of <u>theirs</u>.
9. Open <u>crates,</u> each with <u>its</u> contents intact, cluttered my grandmother's attic.
10. Punctuation correct.

EXERCISE 3, p. 338

The sentences are sample answers.

1. they're
    <u>They're</u> at the front door now.
2. he's
    <u>He's</u> not heavy; <u>he's</u> my brother.
3. she'll
    <u>She'll</u> speak her mind.
4. isn't
    <u>Isn't</u> that your cousin?
5. can't
    <u>Can't</u> you tell anything?
6. shouldn't
    We <u>shouldn't</u> ask.
7. hurricane of '62
    The recent storm was nearly as bad as the <u>hurricane of '62</u>.
8. we'd
    <u>We'd</u> prefer you did not ask.
9. won't
    The door <u>won't</u> budge.
10. aren't
    <u>Aren't</u> you glad you use no deodorant?

EXERCISE 4, p. 339

1. <u>Their</u> hope for financial aid was dashed.
2. Punctuation correct.
3. <u>It's</u> a wonder that any rivers remain unspoiled.
4. The college will grant you admission whenever <u>you're</u> ready.

5. Punctuation correct.
6. The Soltis, <u>whose</u> daughter was married last year, retired to Florida.
7. Now, months after the flood, <u>they're</u> finally moving back home.
8. When <u>its</u> star halfback was injured, the team fell apart.
9. The only way of avoiding a fine is to pay <u>your</u> taxes on time.
10. The children know <u>it's</u> time for bed when the clock strikes eight times.

EXERCISE 5, p. 340

The sentences are sample answers.

1. <u>and</u>'s
   It's easy to use too many <u>and</u>'s in writing.
2. <u>q</u>'s
   She writes her <u>q</u>'s with flourishes.
3. <u>if</u>'s
   That's too many <u>if</u>'s.
4. <u>4</u>'s
   Form your <u>4</u>'s clearly.
5. <u>stop</u>'s
   His job was to paint all the <u>stop</u>'s in the parking lot.

EXERCISE 6, p. 340

Landlocked Chad is among the <u>world's</u> most troubled countries. The <u>peoples</u> of Chad are poor: <u>Their</u> average per capita income equals $73 a year. No more than 15 percent of <u>Chad's</u> population is literate, and every thousand people must share only two <u>teachers</u>. The natural resources of the nation have never been plentiful, and now, as <u>it's</u> slowly being absorbed into the growing Sahara Desert, even water is scarce. <u>Chad's</u> political conflicts go back beyond the turn of the century, when the French colonized the land by brutally subduing <u>its</u> people. The rule of the French--<u>whose</u> inept government of the colony did nothing to ease tensions among racial, tribal, and religious <u>groups</u>--ended with independence in 1960. But since then the <u>Chadians'</u> experience has been one of civil war and oppression, and now <u>they're</u> threatened with invasions from <u>their</u> neighbors.

Chapter 24   Quotation Marks

EXERCISE 1, p. 342

1. "She tells us, 'Dance is poetry,'" Marsha said, "but I don't understand what she means."
2. Mark Twain quipped, "Reports of my death are greatly exaggerated."
3. "We shall overcome," sang the civil rights workers of the 1960s. I think we should still be singing those words.
4. Correct without quotation marks.
5. "Now that spring is here," Ms. Radley said, "we can hold classes on the lawn."

EXERCISE 2, p. 344

Sample answers:

1.   "Do you have the tickets?" she asked as they parked the car and started up the steps through the crowd.
        "Of course," he said. "What do you think I am?" He stopped despite the crowd, patting his pockets. "Oh, no! My wallet!"
2. Do you know a poem that begins, "What is so rare as a day in June"?
3. The sonnet begins: "The world is too much with us; late and soon, / Getting and spending, we lay waste our powers."

   The sonnet begins:

        The world is too much with us; late and soon,
        Getting and spending, we lay waste our powers.

4. Everyone should know by heart the first article of the Bill of Rights:

        Congress shall make no law respecting an
        establishment of religion, or prohibiting the
        free exercise thereof; or abridging the free-
        dom of speech, or of the press; or the right
        of the people peaceably to assemble, and to
        petition the government for a redress of
        grievances.

EXERCISE 3, p. 345

1. "Doom" (or Doom) means simply judgment as well as unhappy destiny.
2. The article that appeared in Mental Health was titled "Children of Divorce Ask, 'Why?'"
3. The encyclopedia's discussion under "Modern Art" filled less than a column.
4. In Chapter 2, titled "The Waiter," the novelist introduces the villain.
5. The Rolling Stones perform "Satisfaction" at almost all their concerts.

EXERCISE 4, p. 347

1. In King Richard II Shakespeare calls England "This precious stone set in the silver sea."
2. The doctors gave my father an electrocardiogram but found nothing wrong.
3. The commercial says, "Aspirin will relieve the pain of neuritis and neuralgia"; but what are they?
4. In his three-piece suit he looked like a real man about town.
5. Poe's story "The Tell-Tale Heart" has terrorized more than a few readers.
6. Years ago an advertising campaign said, "The family that prays together stays together"; today born-again Christians are saying the same thing.
7. "You--come here!" David commanded.
8. Punctuation correct.
9. Must we regard the future with what Kierkegaard called "fear and trembling"?
10. My son asked, "What sort of person would hurt an animal?"

EXERCISE 5, p. 348

In one class we talked about two lines from Shakespeare's "Sonnet 55":

Not marble, nor the gilded monuments
Of princes, shall outlive this powerful rime.

"Why is this true?" the teacher asked. "Why does Shakespeare's 'powerful rime' indeed live longer than 'the gilded monuments / Of princes'?" She then asked if the lines were protected only by Shakespeare's status as our greatest writer. _"No,"_ said one student. _"It has more to do with the power of the language."_ Then another student added, _"Even though paper is less durable than stone, ideas are more durable than monuments to dead princes."_ The whole discussion was an eye opener for some of us (including me) who had never given much credit to rhymes or the words that made them.

Chapter 25   Other Punctuation Marks

EXERCISE 1, p. 351

1. He concluded with an ultimatum_:_ "Either improve the mass transit system, or anticipate further decay in your downtown area."
2. He based his prediction of the Second Coming on John 21_:_17–30.
3. She left her cottage at 8:00 in the morning with only one goal in mind_:_ to murder the man who was blackmailing her.
4. After providing a general view of the harbor, the author then describes_the deck of the ship, its rigging, and the men on board.
5. The Pilgrims had one major reason for coming to the New World_:_ they sought religious freedom.

EXERCISE 2, p. 353

1. The religious--I should say fanatic--quality of their belief was almost frightening.
2. The three cats on the ledge--one Persian, one Siamese, and one Manx--make a pleasant late-afternoon picture.
3. Carnivals, circuses, rodeos, amusement parks--all the wonders of childhood Joey had seen.
4. "The dream just--" she paused, then continued slowly. "Actually it terrifies me."
5. To feed, clothe, and find shelter for the needy--these are real achievements.

EXERCISE 3, p. 355

1. Our present careless use of coal and oil will lead to a
    series of unpleasant events: (1) all of us will have to
    cut back drastically on our use of resources; (2) only
    the rich will have access to these resources; and (3) no
    one will have access to them for they will be exhausted.
2. Some exotic pets (monkeys and fragile breeds of dogs)
    require too much care to be enjoyable.
3. Charles Darwin's On the Origin of Species (1859) remains
    a controversial book to this day.
4. The Rocky Mountains (and they are rocky) look ominous as
    well as beautiful.
5. The Hundred Years' War (1337-1453) between England and
    France was not a continuous war but a series of widely
    spaced battles.

EXERCISE 4, p. 357

1. "The most common trait of all primitive peoples is a
    reverence for the life-giving earth, and the native
    American shared this elemental ethic: the land was alive
    to his loving touch, and he . . . was brother to all
    creatures."
2. "The most common trait of all primitive peoples is a
    reverence for the life-giving earth, and the native
    American shared this elemental ethic: the land was alive
    to his loving touch, and he, its son, was brother to all
    creatures. . . . During the long Indian tenure the land
    remained undefiled save for scars no deeper than the
    scratches of cornfield clearings or the farming canals
    of the Hohokams on the Arizona desert."

EXERCISE 5, p. 358

1. The old Sorensen mansion has all the qualities of a
    building destined for demolition: it is vacant, it is
    decrepit, the taxes on it are high, and the land under
    it is immensely valuable.
2. "Barbra Streisand's sole talent . . . is singing."
3. "Buy the new Universal Dictionery [sic]," the ad said.
    But how could anybody buy a dictionary that can't spell
    dictionary?
4. James Joyce's Ulysses (first published in 1922) is a
    beautiful, shocking novel. (Dashes would also be

possible, but parentheses are preferable to dashes because they de-emphasize a digression.)

5. The sudden warmth, the palest green, the splashy, cleansing
   rain--these signs of an eastern spring were what she missed
   most in California.

6. In the letter he quoted two lines of poetry that John
   Donne once wrote in a letter of his own: "Sir, more than
   kisses, letters mingle souls; / For thus friends absent
   speak."

7. Punctuation correct.

8. Paying taxes--one of life's certainties--is only a little
   less painful than the other certainty. (Dashes are
   preferable to parentheses because they give the phrase
   greater emphasis.)

9. Punctuation correct.

10. The caged gorillas--gigantic and glaring at their sur-
    roundings--seem more vicious than they really are.
    (Dashes are preferable to parentheses because they give
    the phrase greater emphasis.)

Part VI

MECHANICS

Chapter 26   Capitals

EXERCISE, p. 365

1. The building is too tall. It dominates its neighbors.
2. The Grand Canyon is in Arizona, not too far from Phoenix.
3. Capitalization correct.
4. My grandmother never approved of Uncle William's choice of career.
5. The Bible, Koran, and Bhagavad-Gita are the holy books of Jews and Christians, Moslems, and Hindus, respectively.
6. The text for my psychology course, A Study of Psycho-Social Development, opened my eyes about how children learn.
7. Our scavenger-hunt map directed us two blocks southeast and two blocks northeast to find an old sink.
8. The Suwannee River rises in the Okefenokee Swamp and moves through Georgia and Florida to the Gulf of Mexico.
9. The new Saunders Theater is an acoustical triumph, but, oh, it was expensive to build.
10. Never one to take sides, Father says that both General Douglas MacArthur and President Harry Truman were fine men and it's just too bad they had to argue.

Chapter 27   Italics

EXERCISE, p. 369

1. The clock has long since been stolen, but the sign below its old spot still reads tempus fugit.
2. Both the Old Testament and the New Testament of the Bible offer profound lessons in human nature.
3. Esquire was the forerunner of magazines like Playboy, Penthouse, and GQ.

4. No matter how many times I say it, the word <u>euphemism</u> comes out wrong.
5. The <u>Chronicle</u> and the <u>Examiner</u> are San Francisco's major newspapers.
6. <u>Homo sapiens</u> has evolved further than any other species.
7. When Elizabeth Taylor and Richard Burton fell in love while filming <u>Cleopatra</u>, their romance was described as <u>une grande passion</u>.
8. According to the <u>Chronicle of Higher Education</u>, enrollments in business courses are climbing rapidly, whereas enrollments in the social sciences and humanities are plummeting.
9. The mountains were so beautiful that I had to force myself to leave them.
10. Whether he's watching <u>Masterpiece Theatre</u>, <u>Wide World of Sports</u>, or the silliest situation comedy, Larry is happy in front of the television.

Chapter 28   <u>Abbreviations</u>

EXERCISE 1, p. 374

1. They bought a house with <u>one</u> (or <u>a</u>) <u>hundred feet</u> of lake frontage.
2. Mount Vesuvius erupted in <u>A.D.</u> 79 and buried Pompeii.
3. Abbreviations correct.
4. The city built a new office building at the corner of Juniper and Cowen <u>Streets</u>.
5. A dictionary--<u>for example</u>, <u>The American Heritage Dictionary</u>--will tell you whether to punctuate an abbreviation with periods.
6. FDR died on <u>Thursday</u>, <u>April</u> 12, 1945, in Warm Springs, <u>Georgia</u>.
7. The Lynch <u>brothers</u>, <u>William</u> <u>and</u> <u>Robert</u>, went bankrupt in the same year.
8. Abbreviations correct. It would also be correct to omit periods from the abbreviations: USA and USSR.
9. They asked the <u>reverend</u> to marry them on horseback.
10. There, in the middle of <u>Chapter</u> 6, between <u>pages</u> 128 <u>and</u> 129, was a leaf my mother had pressed as a child.

EXERCISE 2, p. 374

The advantages of a <u>graduate</u> degree are not lost on
me. With a Ph.D. I might become a college <u>professor</u>, a
job that would allow me to work only in the <u>afternoon</u>, so
I wouldn't have to get up before 11:00 A.M., and only on
<u>Tuesday</u>, <u>Wednesday</u>, and <u>Thursday</u>, my favorite days. Or
I could get an M.D. and become a <u>doctor</u>. Though I might
have to work long <u>hours</u>, I could earn plenty of <u>money</u> and,
by serving on a professional association like the AMA,
could have a lot of influence. I know about these
advantages because my two older <u>brothers</u> are Prof. Giordano
and Dr. Giordano. I also know how hard they had to work
for their degrees, so I think I'll stick with <u>political</u>
<u>science</u> courses and look for a nice, safe <u>government</u> job
after I get my B.A.

Chapter 29   <u>Numbers</u>

EXERCISE, p. 377

1. A liter is equal to almost <u>1.06</u> quarts.
2. Not until page <u>99</u>, in the middle of Chapter <u>5</u>, does the
   author introduce the main character.
3. Numbers used appropriately, although <u>May 15</u> is also correct.
4. Number used appropriately, although <u>$24.00</u> is also cor-
   rect.
5. Dominating the town's skyline was a sign that stood <u>30</u>
   feet off the ground and measured 112 feet by <u>37</u> feet.
6. <u>One hundred and sixty-six</u> people in the county installed
   some form of solar-heating system in their homes this
   year. <u>Or rewrite:</u> <u>This year 166</u> people in the county
   installed some form of solar-heating system in their
   homes.
7. Outside <u>27</u> Ogden Street, the mayor's house, over <u>150</u>
   people were demonstrating.
8. Number used appropriately.
9. The new school cost <u>$1.75 million</u>. <u>Or:</u> The new school
   cost <u>$1,750,000</u>.
10. Because of the snow, only <u>210</u> students attended the dance.

Chapter 30   Word Division

EXERCISE, p. 380

1. Instead of going to college, she joined the <u>army</u>.
2. Each of the twenty-three apartments he looked at was
    <u>rented</u> before he could make a deposit on it.
3. Americans find any number of ways to keep from feeling
    <u>middle-aged</u>.
4. While the photographers snapped pictures, Dan <u>blushed</u>
    with embarrassment.
5. After the lecture Dotty felt she knew
    <u>enough</u> about the subject to pass the test.

Part VII

EFFECTIVE WORDS

Chapter 31 Controlling Diction

EXERCISE 1, p. 387

Possible answers:

1. The food shortages in some parts of North Africa are so severe that thousands of people have <u>died</u>.
2. A few stockholders have been <u>critical of</u> the company ever since it refused to stop conducting business in South Africa.
3. The most stubborn members of the administration still will not <u>listen</u> to our <u>requests</u> for a voice in college <u>affairs</u>.
4. Though it never became popular, quadraphonic stereo, playing music out of four speakers, <u>provided much fuller and more realistic sound than conventional stereo</u>.
5. I almost failed Western Civilization, because the <u>care-less student</u> who borrowed my notes lost them.
6. We realized after we asked him to cut class with us that he might <u>ruin</u> the afternoon by <u>telling</u> on us.
7. Her arm often aches, but she says it doesn't bother he<u>r</u>.
8. Because he understands <u>politics</u> and can <u>influence the legislators</u>, we should <u>re-elect</u> the governor.
9. Whenever I hear someone boast about the famous people he or she knows, I suspect <u>affectation</u>.
10. The lecture on Charlemagne was <u>fascinating</u>, but I missed some of it because the <u>microphone</u> kept going <u>dead</u>.

EXERCISE 2, p. 389

1. The <u>enormous size</u> of the beached whale--and its horrible stench--both amazed and repelled us.
2. My parents have the <u>illusion</u> that I will enter the family business when I graduate.
3. <u>Credible</u> used correctly.

4. The pond's water was always <u>polluted</u>, so we had to keep from swallowing it when we swam.
5. When students boycotted the school cafeteria, I was <u>uninterested</u> in their childish protest.
6. We've been without furniture for days, but now the movers are due to arrive <u>momentarily</u>.
7. The <u>site</u> for the new bank had formerly held apartments for seventy-five elderly people.
8. <u>Continually</u> used correctly.
9. The <u>effect</u> of the town's hasty decision to close the library has been to deprive poor people of reading material.
10. Having been <u>deterred</u> from acting on impulse, she felt paralyzed by indecision.

EXERCISE 3, p. 390

1. <u>Slumbered</u>, <u>kissing</u>, and <u>bathes</u> all connote gentle slowness in the movement of the river. Related words such as <u>lies</u>, <u>smacking</u>, and <u>showers</u> would connote the opposite.
2. <u>Torn</u>, <u>whirling</u>, <u>intensely</u>, <u>rushing</u>, and <u>immense</u> all connote great violence and magnitude. Weaker synonyms such as <u>separated</u>, <u>turning</u>, <u>very</u>, <u>moving</u>, and <u>large</u> would not convey the same extremes.
3. <u>Bluster</u>, <u>bravado</u>, and <u>flashing</u> connote the swagger of boys. Synonyms such as <u>noise</u>, <u>bravery</u>, and <u>glimmering</u> would not convey the same strutting quality. <u>Meadows</u> connotes idyllic expanses in a way that <u>fields</u>, for instance, would not.
4. <u>Modified</u> connotes a lessening in the strength of principles--a meaning not specifically conveyed by the synonym <u>changed</u>. <u>Pulverized</u> connotes a more tangible sense of destruction than, say, <u>demolish</u>. <u>Center</u>--as opposed to, say, <u>middle</u> or <u>core</u>--connotes a place around which competing forces might move.
5. <u>Swoop</u> connotes a bird's flight; a word like <u>drive</u> would not convey the same speed or ease of motion. <u>Streaked</u> connotes bright color, in contrast to the <u>dark</u> hills; words such as <u>covered</u> and <u>dim</u> would not convey the same contrast. <u>Wheatstubble</u> connotes a low, spiky landscape and intensifies the picture of harvested fields; even <u>wheat stalks</u> would not be so evocative.

EXERCISE 4, p. 392

Possible revision:

I have learned how <u>irritating</u> noise pollution can be since I moved into <u>an apartment forty feet from an inter-state highway</u>. The cars and trucks <u>speeding</u> by make <u>sounds ranging from low rumbles to high-pitched whines</u>, but together they produce a steady <u>roar</u>. Even when all the windows are <u>shut tight</u> and <u>draped with heavy fabric</u>, the <u>roar seeps</u> in through the <u>solid brick walls</u> of the <u>fifty-year-old</u> apartment building. To be heard over the <u>racket</u>, conversation must be <u>shouted</u>, and the television and stereo must be <u>played at maximum</u> volume. Even the <u>hours before dawn are</u> not <u>peaceful</u>, and the <u>roar</u> forms a constant background to <u>fitful, nightmare-filled</u> sleep.

EXERCISE 5, p. 392

Sample answers:

1. fabric, upholstery fabric, velvet
   She chose a wine-colored <u>velvet</u> for backing the pillow.
2. delicious, tart, lemony
   He made a meringue pie, <u>lemony</u> and delicately brown.
3. car, foreign car, Volvo
   He bought a 1973 <u>Volvo</u> station wagon.
4. narrow-minded, prejudiced, sexist
   My uncle's <u>sexist</u> attitudes cause many arguments in our family.
5. reach, stretch, lunge
   Each child <u>lunged</u> for the prize thrown by the clown.
6. green, dark green, bilious green
   The algae covered the surface with a <u>bilious green</u> scum.
7. walk, march, goose-step
   The soldiers <u>goose-stepped</u> menacingly.
8. flower, daisy, ox-eyed daisy
   Some people call the <u>ox-eyed daisy</u> a "brown-eyed Susan."
9. serious, solemn, grim
   His <u>grim</u> expression frightened us.
10. pretty; with small, regular features; with a button nose and a tiny, smiling mouth
    The infant, <u>with a button nose and a tiny, smiling mouth</u>, was a perfect model for baby products.
11. teacher, history teacher, American history teacher
    My <u>American history teacher</u> requires three research papers.

12. nice, considerate, sympathetic
    I need a <u>sympathetic</u> friend.
13. virtue, honesty, frankness
    His <u>frankness</u> was refreshing after I had heard so much
    flattery.
14. angry, furious, raging
    <u>Raging</u> uncontrollably, Andy insulted everyone around him.
15. crime, theft, armed robbery
    Drug addicts sometimes commit <u>armed robbery</u> to pay for
    their habits.
16. smile, closed-lip smile, smirk
    Her contemptuous <u>smirk</u> inflamed him even more.
17. sick, feverish, delirious
    As her temperature rose over 104°, Ellen became <u>delirious</u>.
18. desire, long for, crave
    When my mother discovered that she was diabetic, she
    <u>craved</u> sweets as she never had before.
19. candy, chocolate, Almond Joy
    My little brother would be happy to subsist on <u>Almond
    Joys</u>.
20. misfortune, adversity, calamity
    Losing his sister in the accident was a <u>calamity</u> that
    Jamie could not bear.

EXERCISE 6, p. 394

1. He had waited for years, growing impatient <u>with</u> her
   demands and <u>for</u> the money that she would leave to him.
2. The writer compared gorilla society <u>to</u> human society.
3. They agreed <u>on</u> most things, but they differed consistently
   <u>about</u> (or <u>over</u>) how to raise their child.
4. I was rewarded <u>for</u> my persistence <u>with</u> an opportunity to
   meet the senator.
5. He would sooner part <u>from</u> his friends than part <u>with</u> his
   Corvette.

EXERCISE 7, p. 396

1. <u>Lash of adverse criticism</u> is a metaphor that makes clear
   the words' power to hurt.
2. <u>Blue, limpid boredom</u> is a metaphor that gives boredom--
   an abstraction--some of the concrete qualities of water.
   The word <u>like</u> does not produce a simile, just a literal
   likeness: the pleasure of the state of boredom is like
   the pleasure of lemon or the coldness of salt water.

3. Here are similes: The judge is like a <u>chickadee</u> and the roomful of writers is like a <u>caucus of crows.</u>
4. The metaphor makes a journal, a writer's notebook, a forgotten bank acount.
5. Two similes describe the railroad as a <u>vast fallen empire</u> and as a <u>stodgy, even-dirtier subway, stalled between stations.</u>

EXERCISE 8, p. 396.   No sample answers.

EXERCISE 9, p. 397

Possible answers:

1. These <u>disasters</u> of the war have shaken the small nation <u>severely.</u>
2. <u>The country must choose either to reduce the size of</u> the federal government or <u>to live with</u> having more bureaucrats than citizens.
3. When my father retired from the gas company after <u>thirty years,</u> he was honored <u>by a gift</u> of a large clock.
4. Sam shouldered his way through the crowd, <u>hoping to glimpse</u> the actress <u>he idolized.</u>
5. After years of unprecedented prosperity and nearly uninterrupted <u>peace,</u> Americans <u>now face</u> internal discord and economic confusion.

EXERCISE 10, p. 399

1. When making <u>any plans,</u> one cannot discount <u>chance.</u>
2. <u>Most people</u> are too absorbed in their own lives to care much <u>about others.</u>
3. <u>I like baseball best</u> when the game <u>seems almost over</u> and the home team's slugger hits the winning run out of the park.
4. The attention to detail <u>cooking</u> demands and the creativity it allows are what drew me into cooking school.
5. <u>One drawback</u> of majoring in Asian studies is that, except for <u>rare</u> teaching and curatorial positions, jobs are <u>and probably will remain</u> scarce.

EXERCISE 11, p. 401

Possible answers:

1. <u>Today</u>, security has become a more compelling goal than social reform.
2. Deadly nightshade is aptly named. <u>Its small white flowers become deep black, poisonous fruit the color of night and death.</u>
3. Since the fire that destroyed my apartment also destroyed my books and research notes, I'll have to start <u>my term paper over.</u>
4. The <u>drought devastated</u> crops, but the farmers <u>cooperated</u> to help each <u>other.</u>
5. In <u>his autobiography</u>, and particularly in his version of the Watergate scandal, Richard Nixon <u>merely rehashed</u> old claims.

EXERCISE 12, p. 403

Possible answers:

1. <u>Vandals tore down</u> the new goal posts before the first game <u>and broke</u> windows in the science building.
2. The <u>brightly lighted</u> house on Hedron Street belongs to <u>an ex-madam.</u>
3. I know that <u>politics bores</u> most people <u>my age</u>, but <u>it interests me</u> more and more.
4. When a social reform takes root, such as affirmative action in education and business, <u>a backlash follows</u> from those <u>not directly benefiting.</u>
5. The attendance at the conference was lower than we expected, but evidently the results of the meeting <u>have spread</u> by word of mouth.

EXERCISE 13, p. 404

Possible revision:

After <u>much thought</u>, he <u>concluded</u> that carcinogens <u>could be treated like automobiles.</u> Rather than giving in <u>to a fear</u> of cancer, we <u>should balance the</u> benefits we receive from potential carcinogens (<u>such as</u> plastic and pesticides) against the damage <u>they do.</u> <u>Similarly,</u> rather than responding irrationally to <u>the pollution</u>

caused by automobiles, we have decided to live with them
and enjoy their benefits while simultaneously working to
improve them.

Chapter 32   Using the Dictionary

The answers to the exercises in Chapter 32 depend on the dictionary being consulted. For instance, the recommended desk
dictionaries disagree over nearly half the syllable divisions
in Exercise 1. Thus, no answers are provided for this chapter.

Chapter 33   Improving Your Vocabulary

EXERCISE 1, p. 420

1. benefactor: The root bene means "good," so the benefactor is or does good. The rest of the sentence hints
   that the benefactor provides aid.
2. vacuous: The root vac means "empty," which makes sense
   in the sentence. The heiress takes up volunteer work to
   avoid an empty life.
3. Affixes: The root fix means "to fasten," so affixed
   means fastened.
4. auditory: The root audi means "to hear". The auditory
   nerve is the nerve producing hearing.
5. empathized: The root path means feeling, and the context
   completes the meaning. The child felt as his mother did.

EXERCISE 2, p. 422

1. Quadricentennial comes from quadr, meaning "four," and
   cent, meaning "hundred." The cities will be celebrating
   their four-hundredth year.
2. Octave derives from oct, "eight"; sestet from sex, "six."
   The octave is eight lines, the sestet six.
3. The prefix counter means "opposite to"; a countermeasure
   is one opposed to another measure.
4. The prefix fore means "before"; in trying to forestall
   the squeeze, the representatives are, in effect, trying
   to stall it before it happens.
5. The prefix circum means "around"; circumnavigate means
   "navigate around."

EXERCISE 3, p. 423

The sentences are sample answers.

1. <u>magic</u>, noun and adjective
   adjective: <u>magical</u>
   His success must be the result of <u>magic</u>. Drawing everyone into a <u>magical</u> world, the movie charmed the audience.
2. <u>durable</u>, adjective
   noun: <u>durability</u>; adverb: <u>durably</u>
   The <u>durable</u> chair withstood many years' wear. The <u>dura-
   bility</u> of the old pitcher amazed the crowd. The pup tent
   was light but <u>durably</u> made.
3. <u>refrigerator</u>, noun
   verb: <u>refrigerate</u>
   Don't bother putting that in the <u>refrigerator</u>. It has
   already been <u>refrigerated</u>.
4. <u>self-critical</u>, adjective
   noun: <u>self-criticism</u>
   A <u>self-critical</u> stance is difficult to take. Her apparent
   <u>self-criticism</u> was really a plea for support.
5. <u>differ</u>, verb
   noun: <u>difference</u>; adjective: <u>different</u>
   We <u>differ</u> from each other. He was sure the campaign would
   not make any <u>difference</u>. The police found that she had
   committed a <u>different</u> crime.
6. <u>equal</u>, adjective
   noun: <u>equality</u>; adverb: <u>equally</u>
   <u>Equal</u> rights have not yet been achieved. <u>Equality</u> is the
   goal of a truly just society. The children were all
   punished, though all were not <u>equally</u> at fault.
7. <u>conversion</u>, noun
   verb: <u>convert</u>; adjective: <u>convertible</u>
   We expected her <u>conversion</u> to her new religion. To <u>con-
   vert</u> base metals into gold was the alchemists' dream.
   The <u>convertible</u> sofa comes in handy.
8. <u>strictly</u>, adverb
   adjective: <u>strict</u>; noun: <u>strictness</u>
   She was <u>strictly</u> raised. A <u>strict</u> parent need not be a
   tyrannical parent. The <u>strictness</u> of their morals makes
   the Victorians hard to understand today.
9. <u>assist</u>, verb
   noun: <u>assistance</u>
   Please <u>assist</u> us. Your <u>assistance</u> in this project will
   be greatly appreciated.

10. qualification, noun
    verb: qualify; adjective: qualitative
    The qualification he offered was important. To qualify
    for the Olympics, an athlete must be an amateur. The
    difference between the two tape decks is qualitative.

EXERCISE 4, p. 425. No sample answers.

EXERCISE 5, p. 427. No sample answers.

Chapter 34 Spelling

EXERCISE 1, p. 432

1. brief	6. priest	11. patience
2. deceive	7. grievance	12. pierce
3. receipt	8. fiend	13. height
4. seize	9. leisurely	14. freight
5. foreign	10. achieve	15. feint

EXERCISE 2, p. 433

1. malicious	5. suing	9. suspension
2. lovable or loveable	6. virtuous	10. astuteness
3. serviceable	7. notable	
4. retirement	8. battling	

EXERCISE 3, p. 433

1. implies	5. defiance	9. mistier
2. messier	6. says	10. supplied
3. applying	7. solidifies	
4. delaying	8. Murphys	

EXERCISE 4, p. 434

1. repairing	5. fearing	9. declaimed
2. admittance	6. concealed	10. paralleling
3. benefited	7. allotted	
4. shopped	8. dripping	

EXERCISE 5, p. 436

1. piles	6. boxes	11. librettos or libretti
2. donkeys	7. switches	12. sisters-in-law
3. beaches	8. rodeos	13. miles-per-hour
4. summaries	9. criteria	14. cargoes or cargos
5. thieves	10. cupfuls	15. hisses

EXERCISE 6, p. 442

1. Correct.	8. pre-existing
2. de-emphasize	9. senator-elect
3. forty-odd soldiers	10. Correct.
4. little-known bar	11. two- and six-person cars
5. seven-eighths	12. ex-songwriter
6. seventy-eight	13. V-shaped
7. happy-go-lucky	14. re-educate

Part VIII

SPECIAL WRITING ASSIGNMENTS

Chapter 35 Writing a Research Paper

EXERCISE 1, p. 447. No sample answers.

EXERCISE 2, p. 459. No sample answers.

EXERCISE 3, p. 466

1. Clapham, Abraham, ed. Black Voices: An Anthology of
    Afro-American Literature. New York: New American
    Library, 1968.

2. Anderson, John Q. "The New Orleans Voodoo Ritual Dance
    and Its Twentieth-Century Survivals." Southern
    Folklore Quarterly, 24 (1960), 135-43.

3. Singer, Charles, et al. The History of Technology.
    London: Oxford Univ. Press, 1958. Vol. V.

4. George Segal. New York: Whitney Museum of American Art,
    1979.

5. Bartlett, John. Familiar Quotations. 15th ed. Ed.
    Emily Morison Beck. Boston: Little, Brown, 1980.

EXERCISE 4, p. 466. No sample answers.

EXERCISE 5, p. 467.   No sample answers.

EXERCISE 6, p. 469.   No sample answers.

EXERCISE 7, p. 473

Possible summary:

> Eisinger et al., American Politics, p. 44
>
> Federalism, unlike a unitary system, allows the states
> autonomy.   Its strength and its weakness--which are in
> balance--lie in the regional differences it permits.

Possible paraphrase:

> Eisinger et al., American Politics, p. 44
>
> Under federalism, each state can devise its own ways of
> handling problems, and its own laws.   The system's advan-
> tage is that a state can operate according to its people's
> culture, morals, and wealth.   A unitary system like that
> in France does not permit such diversity.

EXERCISE 8, p. 474

Possible combination of paraphrase and direct quotation:

> Farb, Word Play, p. 107
>
> Speakers at parties often "unconsciously duel" in conver-
> sations in order to assert "dominance" over others.   A
> speaker may mumble, thus preventing a listener from under-
> standing what is said.   Or he or she may continue talking
> after the listener has moved away, thus "challenging the
> listener to return and acknowledge the dominance of the
> speaker."

EXERCISE 9, p. 474.   No sample answers.

EXERCISE 10, p. 476

The exercise instruction says this is a "partial outline,"
and presumably that accounts for the absence of a part II to
balance part I and complete the thesis. Within the given portion of the outline, parallel items are not always worded in
parallel form, divisions are not always logical, and the focus
shifts between the kinds of additives and the functions they
perform. The following is a possible revision, with changed
elements underlined.

    I. Processing, preserving, and improving appearance of
       foods
       A. Processing foods
          1. Causing fermentation
          2. Preventing foaming
          3. Binding ingredients together
       B. Preserving foods
          1. Protecting against internal destruction by
             enzymes
          2. Protecting against external destruction
             a. Bacteria
             b. Fungi
             c. Heat
             d. Moisture
             e. Humidity
       C. Improving appearance of foods
          1. Glazing fruits and vegetables
          2. Causing desirable foaming
          3. Firming canned goods
          4. Thickening texture
          5. Preventing discoloration

EXERCISE 11, p. 477. No sample answers.

EXERCISE 12, p. 480. No sample answers.

EXERCISE 13, p. 490

1.   [1] François Bordes, The Old Stone Age, trans. J. E.

Anderson (New York: McGraw-Hill, 1973), p. 95.

2.   [2] Bordes, p. 121.

3.   [3] Abraham Maslow, "Self-Actualizing People," _Per-_
sonality Symposia, 1 (1950), 26.

4.   [4] Abraham Maslow, _Motivation and Personality_ (New
York: Harper & Row, 1954), p. 34.

5.   [5] Maslow, _Motivation and Personality_, p. 164.

EXERCISE 14, p. 490.   No sample answers.

EXERCISE 15, p. 490.   No sample answers.